Advanced Praise

"This book is *Zen and the Art of Motorcycle Maintenance* for entrepreneurs. It is filled with engaging, instructive, and inspiring stories from Zweig's amazing career, shared with humility, grace, and humor. This 'simple wisdom' is profound, practical, and essential for all aspiring entrepreneurs."
—Michael J. Gelb, author of *How to Think Like Leonardo da Vinci* and *Innovate Like Edison*

"Mark Zweig explains from great personal knowledge what every aspiring entrepreneur needs to know to avoid missteps and ultimately gain success!!!" —Gary Head, CEO and chairman, Signature Bank

"Wow! This book must be a MUST read for any entrepreneurs or those who plan to be. I wish I had read this book twenty-five years ago when I started my business. It probably would have saved us from countless detours we made. Now we operate in global scale, but I still learned a lot from this very enjoyable and fast read. Mark's wisdom is real. It is based on thousands of companies he has helped over years. Nothing like it."
—H. Kit Miyamoto, global CEO, Miyamoto International, Inc.

"This book replaces the how-to with a why-not as Mark Zweig captures the evolution in the life of a real entrepreneur. Zweig's own experiences helped him understand the motivations that drive someone to be an entrepreneur, and he embraces both the challenges and the celebrations that go beyond business and become an exciting lifestyle."
—Dale Carlton, attorney at law, broker, owner, Carlton Realty, Inc.

"Passion creates the drive, purpose develops the vision, hard work makes it happen. These well-articulated simple truths can help guide entrepreneurs in the modern world. This book clearly communicates what you need to cherish to blossom in business, and in life! While the challenges are significant, the fruits of hard work are still worthy of your commitment."
—Jonathan Ward, CEO and lead designer, ICON

T0265474

"If you want to start a business, read this book first! It is a roadmap to success. The return on investment will be more than you can imagine right now." —Burt Hanna, founder of Hanna's Candle Company and Greenland Composites

"I highly recommend this book to anyone thinking of creating their own business. Mark Zweig has a well-deserved record of success as an entrepreneur, and he shares from his vast knowledge and experience. It's filled with practical how-to advice, and he never fails to emphasize the key traits common to success: A positive belief in 'the idea' and a willingness to take the necessary risk. An extremely valuable book for anyone with driving ambition to create a successful business." —Bob Lutz, former vice chairman, General Motors

CONFESSIONS OF AN ENTREPRENEUR

CONFESSIONS OF AN ENTREPRENEUR

Simple Wisdom for Starting,
Building, and Running a Business

Mark C. Zweig

FAYETTEVILLE

2022

ISBN: 978-1-95489-208-8
eISBN: 978-1-95489-209-5

26 25 24 23 22 5 4 3 2 1

∞ The paper used in this publication meets the minimum
requirements of the American National Standard for
Permanence of Paper for Printed Library Materials
Z39.48-1984.

Library of Congress Control Number: 2022941084

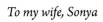

To my wife, Sonya

CONTENTS

Part III. The E-Life

Part IV. Write This on Your Mortarboard

Mark Zweig is a successful entrepreneur and small business owner who has been paying his life lessons forward for several decades. Thankfully, the University of Arkansas (UA) and our surrounding community have consistently been recipients of these lessons. Compiling his insights into this book will no doubt benefit the thousands who read it but also their customers and other stakeholders.

Mark, the full-time entrepreneur-in-residence in the UA's Sam M. Walton College of Business and chairman of Vistage Northwest Arkansas, writes and teaches from his lifelong experience and continual study of business, cares about his students and alumni, and radiates a positive mental attitude. His classes are some of the most in-demand at the Walton College.

As the dean of the UA's Sam M. Walton College of Business, I regularly interact with students, alumni, and business owners who have learned from Mark's wisdom. He helps them network, introduces them to service providers they will need, and pushes them to do things he knows will make a positive difference in their business.

I've not only seen the impact of his advice with others, but I've also experienced it personally.

Not long after we met, Mark challenged me—in his very direct but non-offensive style—to consider several ways the Walton College was too narrowly focused in our approach to teaching entrepreneurship.

For instance, he felt we put too much emphasis in our entrepreneurship-oriented courses on starting a new business and not enough emphasis on buying existing businesses. As he pointed out, entrepreneurship isn't just about starting companies that have a product or service that doesn't currently exist. There is nothing wrong with teaching and encouraging that kind of entrepreneurship, he told me, but it needs to be just one part of the curriculum portfolio.

"You can make a lot of money with small businesses that are in mature markets," he told me. "You just need to provide better service and better marketing."

I knew he was right because I know many alumni of the Walton College who are doing quite well in businesses in mature markets.

He also challenged our focus on technology-oriented entrepreneurship. Again, he was not against it, but he felt like it should just be a part of the bigger picture. And he said we tend to make it sound like owning your own business is riskier than working for a company.

"When you own your own business," he said, "you have many customers, but when you work for a company, you have one customer."

Mark is constructive in his criticisms, and his deep experience on the topics of starting and running a business make him a credible voice. Those are two of the many reasons I listen carefully to him and often ask him for advice.

As you will discover in the pages of this book, he has many creative ways of putting things into new perspectives. And he shares his insights with a very clear writing style that makes his ideas easy to remember and implement.

One tip he doesn't offer, except by example, that I think is worth mentioning is the value of writing about your business. Mark writes well, in part because he started writing at an early age and continued writing throughout all the various businesses he has owned and operated. For him, it is a joy and a discipline.

I've known other successful business owners, like First Orion CEO Charles D. Morgan, who make writing a key part of their approach to leadership. Like Mark and Charles, who also founded Acxiom and wrote *Matters of Life and Data*, I believe writing about what you are doing or trying to do in business helps you become more effective. It is one of the reasons I wrote *The Dean's List: Leading a Modern Business School*.

If I was starting or acquiring a business, I would write about it before it was started or acquired, and I would continue writing about it as I ran the business. So, I'm probably biased, but I think Mark's emphasis on writing is a good influence on our students and on everyone who reads this book.

Of course, this book offers plenty of other practical advice about the ins and outs of starting and running a successful business. But it isn't just about making money. It's also about enjoying the journey and making a difference in the world around you.

Mark is not selfish. He knows how to make money, and he has helped countless other people make money by sharing his time, energy, and knowledge with them. More importantly, his success in business results from adding value that people want and making people's lives better. Ultimately, that's what you will learn from this book. And that's what you will pay forward if you follow Mark's advice.

Matthew Waller, Dean,
Sam M. Walton College of Business

ACKNOWLEDGMENTS

E ntrepreneurs often are seen as lone wolves who roam in search of opportunities to launch, build, and sell businesses with little assistance from those around them. If you've read this book, you know that's not true. Successful entrepreneurs work with a long list of people—employees, partners, investors, vendors, family members, advisors, and on and on.

The same has been true of this book. It would not have happened without the encouragement of Matt Waller, the dean of the Sam M. Walton College of Business—a rare individual who can manage the intricacies and subtleties of leading a business college inside a state-governed institution while at the same time running it like a high-growth business. I also have to say the encouragement and collaboration with my editorial team— Stephen Caldwell and Ryan Sheets—has made my job easy. Stephen, in particular, has done so much to get this book actually done. I can honestly say it would not be done without his efforts. And Ryan has provided an overall direction that has been invaluable.

I'd also like to thank a few very broad categories of people too numerous to name individually—my former colleagues, partners, mentors, and students who all helped me learn the lesson shared in this book. But I would like to single out three of my mentors—all of whom are no longer with us.

Donald Humphries, founder of the Touring Cyclist bike store chain, was super helpful to my early development as an entrepreneur. He was a gutsy guy, originally from West Memphis, Arkansas, and an amazing entrepreneur who risked everything and built his business on a shoestring with very little working capital. He was a great promoter and gave me a lot of freedom to do my job, paid me really well, and let me work as much as I wanted.

Michael Latas, founder of Michael Latas and Associates, hired me right out of graduate school and gave me my first introduction to the architecture, engineering, construction, and development industries. Mike gave me an unbelievable education in selling that has helped me throughout my career. He made me contact CEOs at the age of twenty-two and gave me great confidence that I could do anything.

And the late, great Jerry Allen, former CEO of the company known as Carter & Burgess which is now part of Jacobs, taught me how to keep my cool to better influence others. He was a brilliant entrepreneur who transformed a stodgy old company into a super high-growth, diversified company and was a true "chess player" at business. I can't say enough about the lessons I learned from Jerry while working with him at Carter & Burgess. There are just too many. . . .

Finally, my wife, Sonya—the best partner anyone could have in life and in business. No words could really do her justice. I am a better entrepreneur, manager, leader, and person today thanks to her patience, coaching, wisdom, and guidance. We were best friends and coworkers long before we ever dated or married.

In 2010, I hired her to help me turn around Zweig White (now Zweig Group). I had sold the company in 2004 to a private equity firm, but six years later the lender foreclosed on that firm and asked me to retake the helm. The place was bleeding cash and had a negative net worth. Everything was a complete mess. It seemed like we owed everyone money— printers, hotels, consultants, landlords, and more. Sonya dealt with the lawyers and managers of all these creditors and took care of all of our obligations. She helped organize every aspect of that business, and we were profitable and back on the *Inc.* 5,000 list of fastest-growing private companies by 2013.

She then moved to our design/build development and contracting firm, Mark Zweig, Inc., in the role of "vice president of everything," i.e., general manager. It, too, had suffered from benign neglect, thanks to my focus on Zweig Group and my teaching at the Walton College, and it had a wide range of challenges. She dealt with construction workers who couldn't always understand that a woman could be their boss. She was a whiz with our lenders, found new opportunities for properties to acquire, and upped our game in interior design and client management.

I sold my ownership in Zweig Group in 2018, married Sonya in 2019, and we have been selling down an extensive list of properties ever since. As we ponder our next business venture (if any), we are in the middle of renovating a turn-of-the century house on a large lot on the edge of downtown Fayetteville. With five girls between us, ranging from ten to thirty-four, a one-hundred-and-fifty-pound Great Pyrenees named Gambino, and two cats, Otis and Blanca, we still manage to frequently sit on our front porch together and plot out our next moves.

Because of Sonya and our entrepreneurial ventures, I am living a life many others only dream of—and I strive to be grateful for that every day.

CONFESSIONS OF AN ENTREPRENEUR

From Bikes to a Book:
My Entrepreneurial Journey

Everyone's entrepreneurial journey originates at a unique place, and for some, the specifics fade with the passing of time. But I can trace my story to a street corner in the suburbs of western St. Louis.

I was eight, maybe nine, when I pushed, pulled, and peddled my first bicycles to the corner of North Clay Avenue and Essex Avenue and then sold them to anyone willing to stop and make me an offer.

Bicycles had been a passion of mine almost from birth. I learned to ride not long after I learned to walk, and I got my first bike—a hand-me-down from an older brother—when I was only three. Later, I upgraded to another hand-me-down, and then I got a brand-new AMF twenty-six-inch fat-tired tank cruiser when I was seven or eight. My dad, who had an advertising company, was doing some work for AMF, and he got it for free. It was metallic orange with wide whitewall tires and a built-in headlight in the simulated fuel tank that hung under the top bar.

That one didn't last long, however. I don't recall the details, but it was stolen from the parking lot at Frank P. Tillman elementary school one day when I didn't ride it home after school. Later, we saw some older kids rolling it down a hill and crashing it repeatedly.

I felt kind of bad about it, but, truthfully, it was not the kind of bike I aspired to own. At that time, the Schwinn Stingray and a variety of imitators were just coming out, and my friends and I loved those. Even better were the Schwinn ten-speeds, and I was thrilled when my second-oldest brother, Steve, gave me his blue Schwinn Varsity ten-speed. It was the cheapest Schwinn sold, but it was beautiful to my nine-year-old eyes.

Shortly after I got it, I broke the rear derailleur cable trying to get the slack out of it. I got a new cable from Kirkwood Cycle Shop (they already knew me pretty well by then), but then I stripped the pinch bolt that holds

3

it on the derailleur. So I hopped on the bike and took off for the bike shop. My new cable was long because I hadn't cut it yet, and it clanged on the rear wheel spokes as I sped down the hill. When I looked back to make sure all was well, I ran smack dab into a parked car—a 1965 Chrysler—and landed on the roof with my face looking down into the windshield. I hurt my hand, but worse, I bent the fork and the frame on that Varsity.

Fixing that bike up started my new career. For a more consistent income, I began mowing lawns, and soon I was earning $27 per cutting cycle, but I was always buying broken bikes, fixing them up, and selling them. The AMF was the only bike my parents ever gave me. My inventory came mostly from friends who would give me or sell me their used bikes.

By the time I was twelve, I had taken my first real job working for Kirkwood Cycle Shop, which became my home-away-from home for the next few years. I'll never forget the day my boss showed up with a forty-foot trailer loaded with old bikes and bike parts that he bought from a man who had been running a shop out of his garage. It became my job to fix them up. I paid a kid who was a couple of years younger than me a dollar an hour to strip and sand bike frames that I then painted and decorated with decals I ordered from the manufacturers. We sold some of those bikes on our showroom floor for more than we paid for the entire load. It was fun, and I learned that you could do things at scale and make a profit!

Along the way, I also saved enough money to buy, after significant pleading and cajoling with my parents, a new Sears minibike. The lime-green beauty had a three-horsepower lawnmower engine and no suspension, and I loved it! I quickly started customizing it with chrome fenders, a sissy bar, and a different exhaust.

That purchase opened the door for me to acquire other motorized two-wheelers. One of my schoolmates had a similar Sears minibike that didn't run, so I gave him $5 for the thing, pushed it the two miles home, got it running that night, and sold it a few days later for $27. Then I got a Honda Cub 50 from a neighbor for $13, painted it, and sold it for $65. I also bought a rusty old Sears 106SS that I had seen leaning against the wall of a doorless garage at an old two-family house a couple of doors down the street. I still have the receipt for that $5 purchase. I ordered a parts book from Sears for $2, got it running, and sold it for $50.

By now, I was completely hooked on buying, improving, and selling stuff. I continued to work at bicycle shops, but I also kept my side hustle as the neighborhood's used minibike and motorcycle dealer. I was fifteen when I bought and sold my first car—a 1950 Ford with 31,000 miles on it.

My parents encouraged my entrepreneurial spirit. My father, Fred Zweig, was born and raised in south St. Louis and served with valor in the Sixth Armored Division during World War II (earning the Silver Star and Bronze Star during the Battle of the Bulge). My mother, Evelyn Zweig, married a bomber pilot who died in the war. When my father found out, he rushed back to St. Louis from Europe to court and marry the girl he said he'd been in love with since the fourth grade.

Mom, who turned one hundred in 2020 and still lives in the home where I grew up, was a stable force in our family. She was always on duty, always there to take care of us. She made every meal—we rarely ate out—and kept a perfect house (even ironed the sheets). On top of that, she worked in a variety of jobs. At sixteen, she had a job at Winthrop Chemical Company, and she went on to become a secretary at the National Paint and Wallpaper Association, sell real estate, and eventually run the personal finances for Menlo Smith, founder and chairman of Sunmark Candy Company (and the inventor of Sweet Tarts).

She was emotionally stable, too. She was very even-keeled despite the instability my dad brought into our household. He was always up and down, working furiously on his portable Hermes typewriter, usually without a shirt on, in some room of the house or from a lawn chair in the yard.

Dad, a free spirit, for sure, but someone who dominated the airwaves in our home, founded an advertising agency and was a real-life "mad man," just like Don Draper (in the television show *Mad Men*) but better. In the 1950s, he drove a white Jaguar with red leather interior, and he was a very sharp dresser!

He became disillusioned with advertising in the late 1960s and moved into management consulting. He had a succession of gigs but was mostly interested in human motivation. He studied, wrote, talked, and worked out obsessively. He never worried about money because my mom did that. Dad always told me ad execs died at fifty-seven, so maybe the career change earned him a few extra decades. He lived to be ninety-six and died in the middle of the night.

My parents were an amazing couple, and their words and actions inspired me, my sister, and my two brothers to believe we could do just about anything we put our minds to doing.

For a time, I thought I would become an architect because I loved designing houses on graph paper and then building them with Legos. But the financial payoffs and prestige among my friends that came with all my ventures seduced me into a career in business. So I continued my entrepreneurial pursuits at Southern Illinois University at Carbondale (SIUC), where in four years, I earned an undergraduate degree in business and an MBA.

Shortly after I arrived on campus, I made a deal with a local salvage yard to pick out rebuildable wrecks, fix them up, and sell them by advertising on the student union bulletin board. I also started a moped and motorcycle business with a friend. We got our start-up capital from an SIUC finance professor and split the profit three ways. Plus, I worked as an assistant to the circulation manager at *The Southern Illinoisan* newspaper and had a graduate assistantship during the MBA program that paid me $358.95 a month. All told, I worked at least fifty hours a week while also attending classes.

After college, I went to work for Michael Latas & Associates, a small executive search (and occasional management) consulting firm in St. Louis. Several of my clients were in the architecture and engineering industries. One of them, the Pickering Firm, recruited me, and I and moved to Memphis, Tennessee, to become their director of project development and human resources. I had an ownership stake in the company by the time I was twenty-six. Shortly after, I was recruited to Fort Worth, Texas, by Carter & Burgess (another former client).

In 1988, however, it was time to strike out on my own. My family and I had moved to the Boston area, where I spent a short stint as an executive vice president of a firm before starting Mark Zweig & Associates, a management consulting, publishing, research, media, and training firm that catered to the architecture and engineering industry.

My work with my previous employers and all the connections I had made along the way gave me the foundation I needed to build the business. And what's now known as Zweig Group grew by 30 percent annually for thirteen straight years. Twice it was named on *Inc.* magazine's list of fastest-growing privately held companies.

My role at Zweig Group allowed me to work with several thousand CEOs and managers, mostly in the United States but also in a few foreign countries. I consulted with them on all manner of business issues—strategic planning, leadership transitions, mergers and acquisitions, and marketing, among others.

Then, in 2004, we sold Zweig Group to a private equity firm, Cardinal Growth, and relocated our family to Fayetteville, Arkansas. I began teaching entrepreneurship classes at the Sam M. Walton College of Business, and in 2005 I started Mark Zweig, Inc., a design/build/development company that rebuilt historic homes. It grew rapidly throughout the real estate recession and was named to *Inc.*'s fastest-growing firm list in 2014.

Along the way, I was drawn back to Zweig Group. It was taken over by its mezzanine lender in 2009 and was near bankruptcy in 2010 when I was recruited back in hopes of turning it around. With the help of a friend who is now my wife, Sonya Stout, we got the firm back on track and bought it from the lender in 2012. Zweig Group grew by more than 60 percent between 2010 and 2012 and became profitable again after losing more than $1 million annually.

We sold our interest in Zweig Group in 2018 and started to wind down our development and construction company, which owned about $22 million in investment properties.

Meanwhile, my role at the Walton College expanded through the years until I became an entrepreneur-in-residence full time. In 2021, I also became chairman of Vistage Northwest Arkansas, which provides executive peer groups and coaching.

The writing part of my career evolved somewhat naturally from my role as a consultant and teacher. I have written a weekly editorial for *The Zweig Letter*, a subscription-based industry publication, for more than thirty years, and I am a regular contributor to the *Northwest Arkansas Business Journal* and the *Walton Insights* blog site.

This book is, in many ways, a combination of the entrepreneurial, teaching, and writing aspects of my journey. Matt Waller, my friend, colleague, and the dean of the Walton College, approached me with the idea of authoring a book in 2021 when Sonya and I were researching various small businesses to acquire. We had sold our ownership interests in Zweig Group and were slowly divesting our investment properties, which freed up a lot of time and mental energy.

Matt suggested that the experiences from my career and the lessons I have been sharing for decades with students and other business owners would make for helpful, practical advice to anyone who is running or thinking about starting their own business. So, with the help of two other colleagues at the Walton College, we began combing through my previous writings and pulling together content for this book.

The book is arranged in four parts. Part 1 offers insights and advice to consider before starting a business. Part 2 is about the launch and early growth stage of leading a business. Part 3, the longest section, deals with the various realities of leading and managing an entrepreneurial business once it's up and running. And part 4 provides some parting advice, mainly with graduating students in mind, but it also will offer helpful reminders to anyone who leads a business.

You'll notice that I'm pretty direct and that I often write in lists, numbered or with bullets. There also are plenty of stories to illustrate the points.

As my colleagues and I surveyed the marketplace and discussed the potential value of this project, we found there really was no handbook of this type to help new, aspirational, and existing entrepreneurs with the daily issues they all face. We wanted something simple, easy-to-read, helpful, entertaining, commonsense, and nonintimidating. What you have here reflects our best effort to accomplish that. So read on!

PART I

Before the Beginning

The idea of starting or taking over a business can be intimidating. The unknown is always a bit scary. How do you know if you have what it takes when it comes to skills and personality? And if you can overcome your fears, what do you need to know and do, practically speaking, to give yourself the best chances of success? Those are the types of questions we'll answer in this first section of the book—all the things that you need before beginning your entrepreneurial adventure.

1

There Is No Typical Entrepreneur

There is no such thing as a typical entrepreneur. That's one of the great things about entrepreneurship—it is an option for virtually anyone. There are successful entrepreneurs in every age, sex, race, ethnic origin, and disability category. Some benefit from (and perhaps overcome) a background of privilege, while others overcome (and perhaps benefit from) a background of poverty.

No stereotypes apply here!

Then again, there also are some qualities that bind successful entrepreneurs—qualities not everyone possesses. As you begin to consider whether you might buy or start a business, it is worth it to take inventory of some of the nontechnical attributes that are common among the successful entrepreneurs I have met and worked with over the years.

1. They are passionate about something.

The word *passion* originates from Greek words that essentially mean sacrifice.

Successful entrepreneurs want to fill an unfilled need, help some segment of the population, do something better than it is being done now, or bring something to their area that they think people will want. They are excited about what they do and feel it is a worthwhile use of their time, energy, and money. They are obsessed with their passion and naturally willing to sacrifice for the thing they believe in.

Their passion may border on being annoying to friends and family, but it is through this concentrated thought that they navigate the bloody waters of the marketplace to create a successful business. They know if they aren't obsessed with it, who will be?

One of my best friends, the late Joe Lalli, was chairman and president of EDSA, a landscape architecture firm in Fort Lauderdale, Florida, with

$60 million in annual revenue. Joe constantly talked about his business and its projects. He used to call me every weekend to tell me what was going on, and he worked right up until a couple of days before he died. Why? He had a passion for his business.

2. They know their purpose.

Successful entrepreneurs are driven by purpose. A passion for something may be their interest, but their true dedication comes from a deep-seated sense of purpose. They want to right a wrong. They want to improve the quality of life. They want to contribute to solving a societal problem.

Whatever their business, even those that may seem trivial or unimportant to a casual observer, successful entrepreneurs see how it fits into the greater good, and that is highly motivational to them—and hopefully everyone in their organization.

3. They are willing to work hard—really hard.

Success rarely comes to those who put in a half-hearted effort. Successful entrepreneurs—along with being passionate and purpose-driven—are willing to do the hard work required to achieve their goals. That means work often doesn't shut off at 5 p.m. or on weekends. Things may have to be attended to at all hours of the day or night.

Omar Kasim, founder of Con Queso, Juice Palm, and Plomo Quesadillas (a former student of mine), constantly worked to keep his three businesses thriving in the midst of the restaurant industry-wide COVID-19 slowdown. He personally managed each of his locations and would put in a 100-hour week if needed.

Working those types of hours isn't sustainable, of course, but there are times when it is necessary to get a business up and running or to lead it through a challenging period.

4. They are responsible.

The ideal entrepreneurs take their commitments seriously. They pay bills on time. They don't violate laws. They are honorable. They act ethically. They realize that they have only one reputation and don't want to jeopardize or destroy their future by doing something stupid or short-sighted.

5. They are responsive.

The best entrepreneurs respond to calls, texts, and emails promptly because they don't want problems to fester, don't want to lose business, and know that being responsive shows respect for other people. They know how to treat people so people will like them, respect them, and want to do business with them.

Jim Lindsey, a hugely successful real estate entrepreneur in Northwest Arkansas, was legendary for returning every phone call every day before he went home at night. He often would be the last person in the office so he could accomplish that task because it was something he thought important.

6. They can sell—to clients, customers, lenders, and potential employees.

Like it or not, entrepreneurs have to be effective sellers. That doesn't mean all entrepreneurs must be aggressive cold-callers (although that can be an effective tactic for many businesses). They don't fit the stereotype of being slick, glib, fast-talkers. But they will know how to gain people's trust by being good listeners and problem-solvers and by showing genuine enthusiasm about their business and their products or service offerings.

7. They have high standards that they personally exemplify.

"Good enough" is not the standard that blows people away, so that isn't good enough. Everything has to be done right—at least to the best of their abilities. And they will set that example for everyone else.

I can't tell you how many successful entrepreneurs I know who personally respond to customer service calls or emails so that they are aware of the quality of what their business provides. Dave Weiner, the founder of rapidly growing Priority Bicycles in New York City, is a great example. He mans the customer service desk at times during the day or evening. So does Jay Steinfeld, founder of the $200 million Blinds.com.

8. They can do more than one thing at a time.

Being able to multitask is essential because most entrepreneurs wear many hats in their business, and many different people want their attention and place other demands on their time. You have to be able to juggle your time and your attention.

9. They are constantly curious and always learning.

Learning and improving is a way of life for the successful entrepreneur. That is how they innovate. They stay up to date with what is going on in the world and learn from the experiences of others. They don't hesitate to read a book or seek the advice of others on subjects they feel they need to know more about. They ask questions, attend seminars, and do secondary research. And they are tuned into what their competitors are doing.

10. They are team builders.

Entrepreneurs know how to find good people and how to get them turned on to join their team. They are good with people and have a knack for getting them into the roles they are best suited for. They are good delegators. They know how to make other people feel good about what they are doing. And they are constantly looking for who they want to hire next if they can afford to. It's much like being a professional sports coach.

11. They are relentless marketers and promoters.

You cannot underestimate the importance of marketing, advertising, public relations, and selling in a constantly growing entrepreneurial business venture. During good times and bad, a successful entrepreneur keeps their foot on the marketing gas pedal because they know this is one of the most crucial things they can do to keep their businesses afloat and growing.

If you naturally possess all of those qualities, you will likely do well as an entrepreneur. If one or more of them take you outside your comfort zone, the entrepreneurial life might not be for you.

Then again, it might be that you simply need a willingness to step out of your comfort zone at times. Or maybe with some time, training, and practice, you can grow in areas that right now aren't a strength.

In many cases, these attributes are found in a combination of business partners—one is stronger at marketing, for instance, while another excels at team-building. But some are non-negotiables. If one partner lacks passion or a commitment to high standards, for instance, the business venture will suffer. And while sales might not be a primary function for you, there will be times when you will have to sell to help the business succeed.

2

The Roses and Thistles of Business Ownership

One of the best ways to decide if you have what it takes to be an entrepreneur is to take a realistic look at what it's like to own a business.

Business ownership often is glamorized in movies, TV, and pop culture. There's a tendency to focus on the success stories because people like to hear about the winners, the high achievers, the ones who not only sought fame and fortune but also found it. We see the flower-filled gardens, but, as Brett Michaels sang on Poison's hit record, "Every rose has its thorn."

When things are going well, business ownership can be incredibly rewarding. When things aren't going well, however, it can feel like you've been tied up with ropes and dragged through the thistles.

Fortunately, for most of my forty-year-plus career, the positives have outweighed the negatives. But it's worth reviewing the roses and the thorns before you plant your garden.

First, the roses . . .

Freedom. You are free to associate with whomever you want, to create the team you want, to spend your time (much of it, at least!) how you want, to work with the suppliers you want, to come and go at will, and to work with the clients or customers you want to work with and not work with those you don't.

This freedom is incredibly valuable and is one of the best aspects of being in business.

One of my most treasured freedoms as a business owner is the ability to choose how I want to treat my clients and customers. As the owner, it's your business, and you are in control of what you do, how you do it, and how much of it you want to do. If you believe you need to lose money to make someone happy, then you can do that. This is really valuable if you truly care about people. And who doesn't want to make people happy?

Job creation. Another rewarding aspect of having your own business is the potential to create good jobs for people. You can hire who you want, assign those people their duties and responsibilities, and pay them what you want to pay them. Seeing people respond to the opportunity you have provided and be successful is very motivational to many business owners. It has certainly been one of the most rewarding aspects of business ownership for me.

Financial independence. Not all business owners can claim they have financial independence. But if you are successful in starting and growing a business, it can afford you a virtually unlimited opportunity to make money and build value for the future. And that value could very well be a pot of gold at the end of the rainbow if you build an entrepreneurial venture that can survive. Few—if any—jobs can claim to have the same opportunity for financial independence as owning your own business.

Doing good. The good of a business can be seen in many different ways. In addition to doing something better than your competitors, providing something that is needed in the community, and helping clients, customers, and employees, business ownership gives you a chance to do other kinds of good.

As a real estate developer, for example, I was never motivated by profit. I was motivated by improving the community I lived in. And perhaps your business will allow you to support a particular charity or a cause you are passionate about. When you control where the money goes, you can always make a choice for whatever you define as good.

Those are my favorite flowers that bud by owning a business. You might have noticed that many of them were tied to my desire to help people. Your motives might be different. Some owners are motivated by the challenges of creating processes that solve problems, while others are super goal-oriented and are motivated by achievements—small ones during the journey and big ones along the way. Whatever your primary motive, however, you will have the freedom to pursue it as the owner of the business.

Now for a few thorns . . .

Time. Sure, you can come and go as you like, but you may feel you have to be on duty or on-call twenty-four hours a day to keep the business alive and successful. Especially early on, when you only have a few employees, and you are both the chief cook and bottle washer.

You have to do what needs to be done when it needs to be done, so for some—and many of those who eventually are most successful—there may be some seventy- to eighty-hour workweeks (or more).

Stress. Meeting a large payroll or having huge rent obligations or payments on loans to finance the growth of your enterprise—when coupled with those long work weeks and always being on-call—can create a lot of stress. If you aren't good at dealing with that, a wide variety of problems can develop, including mental health issues, problems in your family relationships, and even physiological health problems.

The chance of public failure. In 2020, more than 4.4 million new businesses were created in the United States—a 24.3 percent increase over 2019, according to the Census Bureau.[1] If the trends recorded by the Bureau of Labor Statistics hold true, however, approximately 20 percent of the small businesses failed within the first year. And within a decade, only 30 percent of those 4.4 million would still be around. That's a 70 percent failure rate.

This doesn't mean you have to be one of the failures. The cause can usually be pinned on one or more big missteps the business owner makes, and this book hopefully will help you avoid some of those pitfalls. But sometimes, even in spite of their best efforts, business owners fail. That can be incredibly embarrassing. And the longer you have had your business and the more well-established it is, the more embarrassing it can be. If your ego is so big that you can't tolerate failure, then you can find such a failure crippling to your self-esteem.

People problems. Consultants love to ask business owners what keeps them up at night. For me, the answer always involves people problems. Two good people who don't get along but should. People who are mistreating other people and may not be aware of it. People who expect to do better than they are. Customers we care about who aren't happy with us. Employees we know we need to let go but feel sorry for.

---

1. Jimmy O'Donnell, Daniel Newman, and Kenan Fikri, "The Startup Surge? Unpacking 2020 Trends in Business Formation," Economic Innovation Group, February 8, 2021, https://eig.org/the-startup-surge-business-formation-trends -in-2020/#.

These are some of the most angst-producing problems, and you seem to have a lot of them when you own a business. They sure don't feel like opportunities when you are going through them.

Financial sacrifices. Most people I know who start a business—especially those coming from good jobs—have to cut their personal overhead. You just can't make as much at first in most cases.

I can remember making $102,000 a year before I started my business in 1988—what seemed like a good living at the time. But I paid myself a base salary of $24,000 during my first year in my new business. That was a huge step down for my family. Out with my new Alfa Romeo, and in with a $200 rusty Dodge Colt. And I'm a car guy!

Plus, your credit takes a hit. Try getting a low-interest, secondary market home mortgage when you are newly self-employed. It may take years. We cut everything and lived in the second-cheapest house for sale in the entire town of Natick, Massachusetts, which we started gutting and renovating completely by ourselves at night.

Fortunately, my business quickly got up to speed, and before the year was over, I earned as much as I had in my previous job. But I held my salary level for years and reinvested the extra money in the business to make it grow. We weren't living large for quite a while.

Family problems. Your family gets involved, whether they want to be or not! I'm not even talking about hiring them to work there—something most business owners do that is fraught with all kinds of peril. But they also may need to make financial sacrifices, or your spouse or kids may have to pick up more of the household chores—any number of things that they didn't necessarily sign up for. (More on this in chapter 15.)

You can't share your political views. We live in a free country, and free speech is one of our rights, so, yes, you can share your political views—if you don't mind alienating half of your clients, customers, and employees. We live in a divided country, so the risk is great.

Many people like to get political on social media, with their yard signs, or with their business communications. But no matter how certain you are of your position on anything remotely political, you will find other people who are equally certain of their position in opposition.

As a business owner, you probably cannot afford to immediately write off half of your potential customers. The one time I strayed into something in our newsletter that was, at best, tangentially political in nature,

I regretted it. All kinds of vitriol came in via mail and fax, and I learned my lesson.

You can't quit. That may seem obvious, or maybe it isn't. But there's no one to turn your notice into when you are the owner of the business. And as the payroll and overhead commitments grow, many business owners feel trapped by their own business. It's good to always know what your exit options are and to keep those in mind as you build so you don't end up feeling stuck in a life that consistently leaves you feeling unhappy.

If you do a quick review, it might seem like there are more thorns than flowers in this garden. But who is to say these items each have the same value? I have always felt the pluses outweigh the minuses. If I didn't feel that way, I wouldn't have done it—and wouldn't still be doing it!

3

Traps, Myths, and Barriers

Entrepreneurs are kind of like artists.

Have you ever noticed that every seven-year-old is an artist, but very few twenty-two-year-olds can draw much more than a stick figure? And most seven-year-olds also are entrepreneurs—selling lemonade, girl scout cookies, or maybe becoming a YouTube sensation. But few adults are entrepreneurs.

Somewhere along the path of life, people seem to lose their entrepreneurial spirit in much the same way that they stop coloring with that big box of crayons and settle for a black ink pen.

I wasn't the only kid in St. Louis who looked for ways to make a few bucks as a preteen, but, unlike most people, I never stopped pursuing new ventures. I just kept doing that kind of thing throughout my whole life. I'm in my sixties and still doing it. Just a couple of weeks ago, I bought a bunch of old Italian motorcycle parts that I turned around and sold to a guy in Philadelphia who, at the time, had more Benelli motorcycle parts for sale on eBay than anyone. Someone gave me a 1964 Honda 305 Superhawk motorcycle, and I plan to get it running and sell it for at least $1,000, maybe more.

I do it because it's fun. It is definitely not the best use of my time. But I told my wife it makes me feel like a kid again.

So why do some people put away their metaphorical box of crayons while others keep looking for a new canvas to paint? I talk about this often with entrepreneurs and would-be entrepreneurs, and every year I ask my students what they learned about starting a business that surprised them the most. I believe many people who would make great business owners get snared by traps, buy into myths, or get stopped by barriers involving entrepreneurship.

The Traps

Our parents discourage it. A large portion of our undergraduate students at the University of Arkansas (UA) are the first in their families to go to college, including many of my students at the Sam M. Walton College of Business.

Their parents all want the best for their children. If Jessica or Jayvon can get a degree and a job in corporate America that starts out paying $60,000 or $70,000 or even more a year, the last thing they think their kid should do is try to start their own business flipping houses or selling pizzas.

They may think, "That's a lot of hard work and would be a waste of your college education." So, they discourage their children from taking the plunge and doing something on their own. And of course, once their off-spring gets that first job, gets married, buys a house and finances it, buys vehicles and finances them, incurs a mountain of other debts, and has their own children, it gets harder and harder to ever step back income-wise and get a business off the ground. So, it never happens.

We are unable to delay gratification. The ability to delay gratification is one of the most critical qualities for entrepreneurs, yet it is severely lacking in many people. We want what we want, and we want it now.

It doesn't help that credit is so widely available for virtually anything you want. When I first got out of school, I was tired of feeling poor as a college student. The first thing I did when I got my first professional job was get married and build a new house that was far more expensive than anything I should have bought. Fortunately, I was able to sell it when I took a new job in another city. But then I did the same thing. Finally, when we made our third move and bought our third house, we wised up and spent less than half of what we "qualified" for.

If you can't stop going out to eat, buying new cars, and taking vacations you shouldn't take, then you will never have the breathing room you will likely need to either start a new business and get it off the ground or the cash to buy one.

Our friends aren't doing it. I see some of the jobs and starting salaries our best new graduates get, and it blows me away. Many graduates move to cool cities to work for great companies in some pretty exciting roles. Then you see how they are living—going out to eat at great restaurants and taking weekend beach vacations—and you can't blame them for taking a job.

If the people in your social circle during this stage in life are doing this, it's natural for you to think you should take that route, too.

There is nothing wrong with that—if you take the right job in an industry you love, keep your overhead low, sock some money away so you can have new options later, and view the whole thing as part of your continuing education. But most people don't do that.

We think about what can go wrong rather than what could go right. People think owning a business is risky; they liken it to jumping out of a plane without a parachute. So take a parachute—and enjoy the view!

Life is full of risk. We take a risk when we do anything—cross the street, eat a burger, get out of bed—but we also take a risk when we do nothing. Risks are inherent in life because so much of life is out of our control.

It's been said that the only things we really control are our attitude and our effort. By focusing on what can go right, we are inspired and willing to address those things that might go wrong so we can prevent them or mitigate them.

The Myths

We think we have to invent something or do something that's never been done. This is such an unnecessary hurdle. The preponderance of business start-ups don't involve inventing anything new. Instead, they try to do something better than existing providers. Or they bring something to a particular audience that wasn't readily available prior to their start-up. Or they simply do something other providers are already doing, but they are in a growth market where demand is greater than supply.

We believe technology is the only start-up option with real growth potential. Again, not true. Many nontechnology-based businesses are profitable, growing, and have tremendous value for their founders and owners to harvest upon exit. There are a ton of examples just within a few miles of the UA campus—Sam's Furniture, Slim Chickens, Fayettechill, Riffraff, Superior Auto Group, Brown Boys Roofing, Rausch Coleman, and Eureka Pizza, just to name a few.

That's not to say there is anything wrong with starting a tech business. And given the number of engineers and computer science majors who are taking entrepreneurship classes, I suspect plenty of additional new tech-based start-ups will pop up in the future. But tech is but *one road* for entrepreneurs, not *the road*.

We think we have to sell our idea to venture capitalist (VC) or angel investors. This is one of the biggest myths. The typical thought process for newcomers to the start-up world goes something like this: Step 1: Create a new idea or invent something new. Step 2: Create a business plan (hopefully, this is step 2, but sometimes this one is skipped!). Step 3: Go "pitch" the idea to potential investors.

Very few businesses, however, start with VC money or angel equity investor capital. Most are started with personal savings, credit cards, and loans from family or friends. For those who are resourceful and create the right business plan, bootstrapping tactics can be used to minimize start-up capital requirements.

We think starting a business is riskier than working for someone else. I have always disagreed with this notion. In fact, I think the bigger risk comes with working for someone else. Maybe it's because I once was fired when, by any standard, I was doing a good job.

Client concentration risk, something we talk about in business school as a factor that devalues your business, applies in this context. As a business, you want a client portfolio that's large enough and diverse enough to survive the loss of any one client. But working for someone else is like being self-employed and having only one client or customer. Lose that client or customer, and you are out of business! Why devalue yourself by placing all your eggs in one basket?

If you start a service or other business that doesn't take much, if any, start-up capital, your risks are pretty low and your success (and continued employment) is tied more directly to how well you perform and not, for instance, on whether management decides to get out of a market or stop doing a function internally that renders you expendable.

We think we're not good enough at a skill we see as necessary to start and run a business. No one is good at everything, so you aren't alone. The key lies in putting the right team together. And everyone you bring in does not have to be a full-time employee or even any type of employee, for that matter.

Many businesses outsource everything from product design to marketing to accounting to IT. It just takes some thought and effort to explore what your options really are.

If you decide to build a team with other partners or employees, you need to focus on adding people with skills and connections you don't have. That's what makes it all work. Don't fall into the trap of only finding people like yourself or those who will be good order takers. That is a recipe for disaster.

We think starting a business requires a vow of poverty. I often hear from students who believe most new business owners can't pay themselves anything for years. They think they must work sixteen hours a day, seven days a week for years before getting any payback and that they can't have a family or any personal life if they own their own business. Furthermore, they believe all entrepreneurs go broke at least once before becoming successful.

Starting a business is hard work that demands sacrifices, especially in the short run. But when it's done the right way, you don't have to live on noodles and water. Not only can it provide a good living on a daily basis, but it's also an investment in the future. So you not only take out of it what you need to live, but you can also extract more value later if you sell the business (one of the primary tenants of entrepreneurship).

The Barriers

We don't know where to start to create our own business. This can be a legitimate barrier, but it's one that anyone can overcome. There are a great many resources available today that can help you figure out what business to go into, test a concept to see how the target market responds before making a major commitment, create a plan, and finance a business.

Here in Northwest Arkansas, for instance, the Arkansas Small Business and Technology Development Center, Startup Junkie, and StartupNWA all provide free consulting, programs, events, and other services to help budding entrepreneurs. The McMillon Innovation Studio at the UA brings together students, faculty, and business leaders from across disciplines. And the Brewer Family Entrepreneurship Hub provides training, coworking space, and other services for new and early-stage entrepreneurs. Other cities have similar resources.

We are too young or too old to start a business. The great thing about entrepreneurship is that the door is open to all. There are ten-year-olds starting businesses, and there are eighty-year-olds doing it. I have businesses and a full-time job, but I would still consider starting a new venture right now.

There are good reasons (as I'll cover in chapter 4) for starting a business when you are young, but you are never too old to take the leap. The key is to pick a business and develop a plan that works for you—one that matches your skills, interests, and passions with real needs that exist in the market and one that you can afford to do.

Everyone has the option of starting a business if they really want to! Maybe it's time to pull those crayons out and create a masterpiece worthy of showing off on your refrigerator. I'll bet you would be better at it than you think!

A Mo-Better Idea

I have mentored dozens of students who wanted to start their own business or who had already done so and needed some help with it. And the truth is, I sometimes still fall victim to some of these traps, myths, and barriers when offering my advice and opinions.

For instance, I will never forget Mo Elliott, founder of the eco-clothing brand, Fayettechill. Mo sought me out when he was an undergraduate at the University of Arkansas to get my reaction to his idea of starting a T-shirt company.

I was completely unimpressed by the idea.

"We already have a bunch of T-shirt companies here in town," I thought. "Plus the word *chill* will go out of fashion someday and sound like *groovy* does to us today."

Boy, was I ever wrong. Mo started his company and became wildly successful. He understood his market because *he* was his target customer—a kid from the flat, concrete suburbs of the Dallas-Fort Worth area who came to the University of Arkansas and discovered the Ozark foothills and all of our outdoor recreation opportunities. He sold a lifestyle with his brand, and today he has a company that does several million dollars in sales.

4

The Best Time to Start a Business

I t's been said that one of the truly great things about entrepreneurship is that it is available to people of all ages. In fact, I said that very thing at the end of chapter 3!

Young, old, or middle-aged people all have the opportunity to start or buy a business they can nurture and grow to create value that they can harvest upon exit—one of the primary distinctions of an entrepreneurial venture versus something that is just a small business.

But I've grown to believe that the best time to start a business is as soon as you are ready, and most people are ready sooner than they think.

In my role teaching entrepreneurship at the Sam M. Walton College of Business, I work with a lot of young people—most of them seniors by the time I have them as students. If they know they want to start a business of their own but don't feel ready, I encourage them to take a job in an industry that connects to their passions. They can use the experience not only as an opportunity to make a living and achieve financial independence but also as an important part of their continuing education that will help prepare them to do their own thing someday.

That said, I also encourage them to consider taking their first entrepreneurial plunge while they are still relatively young. There are many reasons for adopting a sooner-than-later mindset when it comes to starting or buying a business. Here are some:

1. Your risk tolerance often wanes with age.

As an entrepreneur who has started a half-dozen boot-strapped businesses, been a minority owner in a half-dozen more, and once had about $20 million in heavily leveraged investment real estate, I have, by most any standard, a high tolerance for risk.

Entrepreneurs, of course, don't really think what we are doing is that risky. We minimize risk through thorough research and market testing.

But at some point, you also become aware that you have a lot to lose. Plus, at some age—whatever that is—you don't have a lot of time left to make up for failed business experiments. Your time to play the game is limited. The older you get, the less likely you are to take a chance doing something that could very well fail.

2. As you age, other obligations take more of your time, money, and mental energy.

Your spouse, your adult children, your grandchildren, your civic commitments, and maintaining all of the stuff you accumulate takes time away from your business. Plus, your financial obligations grow the older you get. Big house payments, a spouse who may have dedicated their best working years to raising a family, college bills, and more can all require more financial commitment from you than a new venture will be able to support early on.

A new, entrepreneurial business is all-consuming. It takes everything you have to make it succeed. It's best to be in a position to really commit if you are serious about doing it.

Baking a Business

One of my students was a junior at the Walton College when he decided he wanted to start a business making protein-rich baking mixes. He was a bit of a fitness nut himself and was convinced the market needed his product. So he and a couple of his friends who weren't students at the UA launched the business. They created and tested products, and they had data that showed their products were superior to others on the market.

While I am not exactly sure what happened to their relationships, let's just say things ultimately didn't work out. The other two partners ended up buying out my student's share of the business for six figures in cash. So now he is a student with a nice chunk of money that he is going to use to start yet another business—most likely a property management company. He is hooked and will probably never work for anyone but himself for the rest of his life.

3. You don't have to quit your day job.

There isn't a thing wrong with starting something part-time to see how the market responds and to see if you really find it fulfilling.

While this isn't always possible because of the time or monetary commitment your new venture might demand from you, it often is, especially with service businesses or internet-based businesses. Even if your full-time job isn't in the same business or industry you want to go into, you will at least have a paycheck while you are testing the market. That will help you live on less and take less out of your business. It will also help you secure credit if you need to borrow money for your venture and reduce your risk of inadequate capitalization.

When you are young, you also might consider working for a business that does what you want to start or buy for yourself. This will not only reduce your risk of failure once you have your own company because of the training and learning opportunities you will have, but it will also help you understand whether you even like that business, which is also critical to your long-term success. And you can learn on someone else's dollar.

4. You are familiar with living on very little.

As a college student or recent graduate, you are probably used to being poor. And all of your friends are likely poor because they, too, have been students. This is an ideal time to start a business because you won't feel like you are missing out on the "good life" of your peers who have paying jobs. It gets harder to live on less as you age. Many entrepreneurial enterprises fail because their owners need to take too much money out of the business so they can maintain their high standard of living. When you don't need a lot of money, it is a great time to try it out.

5

The Gestation Period

Failure often is glorified in the business media. The pundits tell us we are supposed to fail often, that failure is good, and that we should revel in all the learning opportunities it presents.

And sure, there are lessons to learn from failure. Some of those lessons are that it's no fun being embarrassed, letting people down, and losing money—whether that money is yours or it came from people who believed in you and invested in or loaned money to your business.

It's great to learn from failures, but it's even better to learn ways that will help you avoid failure whenever possible. And one of the primary reasons many businesses fail is because they weren't very well thought out. Their founders weren't prepared and made some bad assumptions and decisions as a result of that lack of preparedness.

Fortunately, there are steps you can take before starting a new venture that will help ensure your success—or, as is often becomes the case, provide you with the information that will actually keep you from starting the business.

Business ideas typically need a gestation period, so here are some things you can do as a precursor to birthing a business:

1. Pick the right business.

Some businesses are more likely to succeed than others. Service businesses, for example, cost a lot less to start than others. Some have fewer (good) competitors. Some have an easier time finding workers than others.

You also want to go into a business that has proven demand. If you have invented something new, you need to prove there will be a demand for it. But as I mentioned earlier, you don't have to invent something new. While I don't advocate starting the thirty-second Mexican restaurant in a town that already has thirty-one of them, one thing is clear: There is a lot of demand for Mexican food in that town. So if your idea is truly different and better than what is available, you may be able to expand the market or take business away from the businesses that already exist.

Be smart about what you are going into. There is a lot to be said about an all-new idea, but there are also many pluses associated with going into a business that serves a proven market where you can be differentiated from everyone else.

You also should consider non-start-up options, which I cover in more detail in chapter 6.

2. Pick the right legal form for your organization.

I am shocked by how many founders use LLCs without considering the ramifications of that decision. It seems like 95 percent of founders I talk to either have set up an LLC or are planning to create an LLC.

If you think you will ever add other owners or need outside equity capital, however, my experience is that a corporation that is governed by corporate bylaws and a shareholder buy/sell agreement is vastly superior. Whatever you do, I strongly suggest consulting a specialized attorney who is knowledgeable about the pros and cons of your options.

3. Source your products.

If you are a product-based business, locate as many different sources of supply as you can for whatever you are selling. Contact them to start getting specific prices and lead time estimates for preliminary quantities in the exact specifications you will need.

Ask yourself why these providers would want to do business with you—an unproven upstart—because it's important to think about things from the other person's point of view.

4. Identify your competition.

Figure out who the big players are in the market and understand their target markets, products, services, and pricing models. You need to know how your business fits in and what you will be doing that no one else is. Differentiation versus a "me too" business is where the blue ocean (less competition) will be for you.

5. Bounce your idea off industry experts, customers, and lenders.

Be open to the reactions and advice of people who have experience in the business you want to enter. This step alone could be one of the most important ones you will take in your planning.

These people will know the industry much better than you do. They have likely seen or even experienced successes and failures of specific businesses in that industry. They will understand the environment both inside and outside of the industry that is affecting it. And they could possibly know other people who could be helpful to you. Be smart, and get their input!

Likewise, get input from your primary target customer group. Listen not just to what they say but also how they say it. Are they genuinely enthusiastic about your business idea? If not, where do they see the deficiencies in your planned offerings? Your potential buyers—and their opinions, preferences, and reactions—are the most important people you will need to please. Or guess what? You won't make it.

Finally, talk to lenders and other potential sources of capital, and not just to ask for money. It's best to start getting these people involved early. They will not only appreciate that you did, but they can also give you valuable guidance and input. And you will have a better, more realistic sense of what your actual options will be if you do this.

6. Be smart about debt.

Find every source of debt capital you can before you need it. This may not seem at all profound, but get credit while you can. The best time to do that is when you are still employed and have W-2 income.

There are a wide variety of loan options you can get lined up in advance of the need—lines of credit, equipment loans, home equity lines, credit cards, and personal loans, for instance. Do all of this when you have a job, and you will have a safety net later when you have your own business and have tight cash flow. Once you quit your job and go all-out into your new venture, it may prove to be much more difficult to get credit.

The more credit you can get, the less equity you will have to give away to get the capital you need to get going and survive. I prefer local or regional banks where I can really get to know the top people and they can know me. That personal relationship with your banker can be a lifesaver at times.

Using credit to finance a start-up, however, isn't a license to operate at a deficit. Debt capital—unlike equity capital—will have to be paid back whether you succeed or fail. Make sure the business plan identifies how you will be cash-flow positive, and constantly look ahead to make sure you don't run out of working capital.

It isn't a lack of capital that kills businesses but a lack of discipline and good accounting. In fact, a lack of capital may actually increase your odds of success by forcing you to become scrappy and disciplined from the very start. It can be more of a blessing than a curse.

7. Identify your key service providers.

Start thinking about who your legal, accounting, and other professional services providers will be, and get their input on your idea. There are specialists in every discipline. Find those with experience in the industry you want to enter and those who are committed enough to your relationship to work with a high-growth start-up like the one you are planning to launch. That takes time and dedicated attention. Who will give you that? Work with them.

8. Start sourcing your team.

Start thinking about who you want on your team, either as employees or business partners. The right people make all the difference.

Most new ventures rely on the founders and their friends and family members to fill key roles. There may be some good people in that pot, but then again, there may be some huge personnel problems there, too.

Remember, your future HR problems lie in hiring your friends, family members, and people simply because they will work cheap. I always caution my students on this one. Hiring friends can work out—but if it doesn't, you could lose your friendship. Ditto for family members in the business. Just think about how you will deal with a family member or friend who isn't performing or one that is causing problems for your customers or other employees.

I can't tell you how many people I know personally who are going through these situations right now. One of my former students works for a family business, and they are saddled with a nonperforming former best friend of his father who is working in a key role. They don't know what to do about the problem.

Avoid that type of distraction. Start to build your team by thinking about who would be best in any role you will need to fill, and then bait the hook. Get them interested early. They may have valuable input.

9. Avoid a 50/50 partnership.

There's comfort in going into a new business with a partner or partners, but don't be 50/50 partners with anyone—except for perhaps your spouse. Equal partners often encounter conflicts with no way to resolve them. Someone has to be in charge and have the right and ability to make a decision. Plus, someone will probably devote more time and energy to the new business. (I'll write more on working with your spouse in chapter 15.)

10. Pick the right name.

Picking a name for your business is critical. It seems the trend today is to pick a single word that is unrelated to the business (or at least that isn't obvious at first blush).

For better or worse, I seemed to always have my name in my business. I was pretty well-known in my industry as a writer and speaker even before starting my businesses, and it is an unusual name that people don't hear every day. I figured it would be memorable.

Of course, some would say that using your name in your business glorifies the ego. There is some truth to that. There is also a risk that if something goes wrong, your reputation could be permanently sullied. Everything has its risks, and for me, the reward of quick name recognition and immediate business won out.

Whatever you do, it's important to check the availability of the web domain for the name you want to use. It's best if you can keep both exactly the same because it makes it easier for people to find you, and it makes your name more memorable.

11. Learn the language of business.

For several years, we worked with a Mexican-American painter named Miguel who told me that he encouraged all of his workers to go to night classes to learn English. If they didn't learn the language, he told them, they would be doomed to a lifetime of working for him or someone like him for less than they should be earning. But if they learned the language, they could have their own business someday, just as he did. He also said that if you were an American trying to work in Mexico and didn't speak Spanish, "you would end up either dead or broke, or both."

The same principle applies to the language of business—numbers. Why would someone try to work in business and not understand accounting and finance? It doesn't make sense.

If you own or work in a business and don't understand the numbers of that business, you will not be able to do your job as well as you should. Bad accounting—not paying attention to the available numbers—is one of the primary causes for underperforming or, worse, failing businesses.

My classes at the Walton College contain a mix of business students and those who have majors in other colleges. I would say somewhere between 50 percent and 70 percent of the students who take my classes do not understand what an income statement is, what a balance sheet is, what working capital is, or what a cash flow projection is (and how to do one). Knowing this information is essential to their survival.

I also see this in some of the companies my students work with as a part of our small enterprise management class. These are real businesses, and many of them are struggling financially in large part because they lack a grasp on their numbers. They don't know what their breakeven is. They don't know what they make or lose money on.

If you don't understand this language, get some training. Take a class or find a mentor, but find someone who can teach you about basics such as cash flow, balance sheets, and income statements. And teach the language to your employees. The more you and your team understand the language of numbers, the better you can use that language to your advantage.

6

You Don't Have to Start from Scratch

W hen it comes to entrepreneurship, the emphasis in all forms of media is on start-ups. People love the new—new ideas, new products, new markets, new everything. But abandoning that preconceived notion opens up a whole range of opportunities.

Entrepreneurship is more about value creation than about doing something new, which means there are at least two other doorways to entrepreneurship: purchasing an existing business and buying a franchise. And both can be done in mature, existing markets.

Buying an Existing Business

Existing businesses come with several advantages. For instance, you have historical financial numbers, which makes planning and budgeting easier and more accurate. Rather than trying to predict what an entirely new business will produce, you can already see what costs can be cut to make a profit, what products and services sell the best, and what areas of the business are the most profitable.

An existing business also typically comes with one or more locations, which means you don't have to find the right place to do business. And you already have many of your most important relationships—with employees, suppliers, and clients or customers. Start-ups often underestimate the cost and time it takes to hire and properly train employees or to find reliable suppliers.

If the business has been successful, you also are buying the goodwill that's been created. And existing customers, clients, employees, and suppliers often will have ideas on how to make things better. That's all incredibly valuable as you plot future improvements.

An existing business also already has systems and processes in place. The seller often can provide training to help you understand the ins and outs of the enterprise, which improves your odds of avoiding costly blunders so you can immediately operate at a profit. Even if they aren't doing every-thing the best way possible, they are doing them, and that may make it easier to figure out how to improve them.

In addition to making training a part of the deal, the seller might be will-ing to finance your purchase, in whole or in part. It has been said of buying a business that terms are more important than price, and there's a lot of truth in that statement. Some sellers are highly motivated to get out, so they are agreeable to terms that are favorable to the buyer.

All of these advantages lower the risk for you as an entrepreneur. Of course, there are plenty of ways buying an existing business can go wrong. That's why due diligence and using a good attorney are critical, so you aren't later surprised by the hidden liabilities.

Buying a Franchise

A good "business format" franchise, as opposed to what is referred to as a "product and trademark" franchise, provides a business plan in a can. The franchisors will have facility designs, sources of supply, provide manage-ment and employee training, and much more. You can also talk to other franchise owners and observe their businesses. That will reduce your risk.

My friend Mike Stennett used this as his entry into entrepreneurship. Mike was in his late twenties when he bought a Steak 'n Shake franchise and opened a store in Northwest Arkansas in 2005. He and his wife had saved up $50,000 from his job as a Steak 'n Shake manager in Missouri, and he borrowed another $450,000 from someone who just happened to like the restaurant chain and thought we needed one in the area. Mike then borrowed more money from a bank and built his restaurant near the Northwest Arkansas Mall.

Now Mike and his wife own nine Steak 'n Shake restaurants and three Dickey's Barbecue Pit restaurants. He is still a young guy with lots of energy and motivation, so he has no plans to stop adding more franchise restau-rants to his growing empire.

Mature Markets

Existing businesses and franchises both provide opportunities in mature markets, and that, too, comes with advantages over starting something totally new in an unproven market.

There is something to be said for a market that you are certain exists for whatever it is that you want to sell. There's no mystery or chance that no one wants it when it's beer, furniture, tacos, jeans, house painting, pool maintenance, or any number of other products and services.

In a mature market, you also can see exactly who your competitors are and what they are doing. It is super helpful to see all of the competitors' offerings so you can figure out what works, what doesn't, and what unique niche you can provide that's currently unfilled.

Differentiation and innovation can lead to a breakout. Having really great customer service is always an opportunity to distinguish yourself. That can happen no matter how thinly capitalized you are.

Mature markets also tend to have a strong labor pool because there are other providers of whatever your business is selling. That's good news for you because there will be people who can do what you need to be done.

So you don't have to invent something new to be successful as an entrepreneur. That's one way, but it's not the only way. There are plenty of great opportunities to serve mature markets with an entrepreneurial, growing venture, too.

7

The Value of Outside Directors

The typical privately held business has a board of directors made up entirely of insiders who work in the business. One thing that any company of any age, size, or type can do to help make them more successful is to either add outside directors to their board or add outside advisory (nonvoting) board members to their board.

I will admit that even in my own businesses, I wasn't always in favor of it. Was I afraid of what these people would learn about my firm or about my capabilities as a leader? Maybe. Or perhaps I just didn't want to take the time to go through the trouble of educating them on the particulars of our business. Either way, I was wrong. It's crazy not to do this.

Outsiders provide a truthful evaluation of what is happening in the business. Most outside board members or advisers don't need the job. They can tell the emperor that he or she has no clothes when other people who are also employees of the business might not be willing to do so.

They bring a lot of knowledge and experience to the business because they have been there before, been through crises, and survived. They have grown businesses. They have bought and sold businesses. They have been through management transitions. All of this and more can be invaluable when dealing with these situations for the first time.

They also provide a pool of potential mentors for the CEO. It's lonely at the top. Many CEOs and company founders have no one to talk to who understands what they are going through. The right outside directors can help by providing a go-to resource on nearly any issue the top person is dealing with.

Another advantage of outside advisors is that they often can expand your pool when it comes to marketing, selling, and financing. They can provide access to outside sources of capital, for instance, because they typically know other successful people who might be interested in investing money that could be crucial for the business. Likewise, they can help you get new clients or projects. In several cases, we never would have secured the contract—some for millions of dollars—without the help of the outside director.

Of course, who you pick for an outside board member or adviser is critical. Diversity is one consideration. Too many boards are a collage of white males who are all fifty or older. Adding younger board members, women, and people of different races and cultural backgrounds improves creativity and accountability.

Personally, I have a predilection for people who have been at the top of other businesses in the same industry or who have served at high levels in client or customer organizations. In some industries, having a former or retired regulator can be incredibly helpful. One person I don't usually recommend as an outside director or adviser is the firm's outside accountant or attorney. You already have the input of these people through their paid service arrangements.

What should you pay these outside directors or advisers? I can only tell you about my experiences. When I served in this role, which was mostly with established companies, I was paid between $20,000 and $100,000 annually, plus travel expenses. In one case, the company had only eight or

The Structural Soundness of a Great Board

Miyamoto International, a global structural engineering firm that specializes in designs for buildings in areas prone to earthquakes, traces its roots back to 1946, but it was relatively small when H. Kit Miyamoto joined the firm in 1990. Miyamoto bought the company in 1997 and eventually changed the name as it grew to become an industry leader.

Miyamoto, of course, deserves credit for shepherding that growth, but I also believe the company benefited from one board member in particular. I served on the Miyamoto board for years, but I am talking about Peter Yanev, another early board member. Yanev was the founder of EQE, a very successful earthquake engineering firm that grew to more than eight hundred employees. Miyamoto had fewer than ten at that time. Today it is an international company with offices around the globe. Yanev provided a real blueprint to follow to be successful. What was that worth? A lot!

nine employees, and I took my compensation in stock. The company has performed well and today has more than two hundred employees in about twenty-five offices around the globe. In other cases, I put in some cash to buy stock at a discount. In another case, I was given stock on top of my board fee. And in other cases, I never had any ownership.

I do know that there are some good people who will serve for free, or for $1,000 a meeting, to help get a new business off the ground or where they have a special personal relationship with one or more of the business founders.

No matter what you pay, it will be a lot less than what it would cost you to hire one of these people full time, even if you could. I have served on boards alongside many retired CEOs of larger companies, chairpersons of publicly traded companies, and entrepreneurs who were very, very successful but who were still willing to give back some of their valuable time to help other people become more successful.

In my case, a big part of how well it works is the chemistry with the other board members and the firm's top management. If I don't feel stimulated by my involvement with those people, I won't waste my time on their board no matter what I get paid. I have been on boards where every meeting left me feeling deflated and depleted of energy. In every one of these cases, the company would not do what I thought was necessary to turn their situation around or become more successful, so I withdrew my nomination for another term or resigned. The lesson here is to pick the right outside members in the first place and to be willing to listen to and act (at least sometimes) on their suggestions if you want to keep their interest and enthusiasm.

8

Why You Need a "Fred" as Your Business Partner

I was really fortunate.

In 1988, shortly after I started my first real business—Mark Zweig & Associates (what is today known as Zweig Group)—I found the perfect business partner in Fred White.

Fred was in his late twenties and finishing his bachelor's degree in fine arts when I hired him as a part-time desktop publisher for the firm where I worked as an executive vice president. We had only known each other for a few months when I left to launch my venture, but my then-wife said, "you need Fred" in this business.

I totally agreed.

We invited Fred and his then-wife for dinner in Boston and struck a deal for him to come to work with me. It was late July, and he had gone full time at our prior company upon graduation a few months earlier for $23,500 a year. Our deal for him to join Mark Zweig & Associates was that he would get paid $1,000 a month plus 25 percent of anything we had left after paying expenses for things like our office space, copier leases, and payroll for our other employees. I would get paid $2,000 a month and the remaining 75 percent of the profits.

That may sound unfair, but Fred was just starting his professional career while I was already well-known in my industry as a writer and speaker. I also had finished my MBA eight years earlier, had considerable work experience in my field, and had already been a partner in a firm.

Fred lived in a small apartment in the Back Bay area of Boston and rode his bicycle or took the diesel commuter train all the way to our office in Natick, about sixteen miles west of Boston Harbor.

An artsy, quirky guy by any standard, Fred had graduated high school from the prestigious Phillips Exeter Academy in New Hampshire the same year as its first female student, Jenny DuPont, who years later became my next-door neighbor in Dover, Massachusetts. He then went to the University of Pennsylvania as an engineering and computer science major but eventually dropped out and worked as a warehouseman and line cook at IHOP. He played in a rock band and traveled extensively through Europe before pursuing his fine arts degree at Emerson College in Boston.

Hiring Fred is one of the best business decisions I've ever made. The guy is brilliant—undoubtedly one of the smartest people I have ever known—and he has skills that are completely different from mine. He is a systems-oriented, long-term thinker. He created all of our processes for efficiently turning out original research reports. He created our direct mail marketing system. Most importantly, he created the single integrated client and potential client database that we used to do all our work and all our marketing. It eventually ran on a wide area network and was on every employee's desk.

This allowed our company to grow by an average rate of 30 percent annually for the first thirteen years. It also landed us a spot on the *Inc.* 500 list of fastest-growing privately held companies two years in a row, something less than 30 percent of the *Inc.* 500 companies had done at that time.

A couple of years after Fred joined me, we incorporated our business and issued stock. But it was a 60/40 split versus the 75/25 profit split deal we started out with. It was the right thing to do because he was so pivotal to our success. Fred—a very introverted and self-effacing guy—always kept himself in the background while I basked in the spotlight. But in recognition of his contribution, we changed the company's name to Zweig White. That, too, was the right thing to do.

Over time, we sold stock to more than twenty of our employees, diluting our ownership until eventually selling the business to a private equity firm a little more than sixteen years after starting it. That's when I "retired" and came to Fayetteville, Arkansas, to become a college professor and to start my next business, a design/build/development company.

The point of this story is that none of our success would have been possible without Fred White. He was the best business partner I could have had, and a big reason for that is because we were completely different personalities, had different skills, and had different areas of interest. That meant that we would rarely tread into each other's territory.

We certainly had our disagreements over the years (most of which I'm sure were caused by my stubbornness and need to dominate at that point in my life—not something I'm proud of today), but we shared a common philosophy and vision for what we could do with that business and a desire to build it and sell it at some point. We achieved our goal, although it took us a little longer than we originally planned.

Today, Fred and his wife Audrey own a café in the Jamaica Plain area of Boston, and Fred works as a software developer with an entrepreneurial San Francisco–based company focused on the architecture and engineering industry—the same industry our joint company was entirely dedicated to serving. Although we communicate infrequently, I still consider him a friend and will forever be indebted to him for the contributions he made to our business.

The fact that Fred and I were so different in our backgrounds and skills made for a really good partnership. I didn't always like him, and I'm sure he felt the same way about me. He was difficult to work with at times because he was so much smarter than the rest of us. But I always respected him and appreciated what he did. The mistake so many entrepreneurs make is they team up with someone who is very similar to themselves—not, in my opinion, the best way to go!

The moral of the story for start-up founders is this: Pick your business partners carefully! It will either make you or break you.

9

How to Use Debt Wisely

once read a post on LinkedIn by a popular pundit who describes himself like this: "Leader/Sales Professional/Inspiring the World Through Personal Development and Entrepreneurship." He told a story that was supposed to help readers understand that all debt is bad and that you shouldn't buy anything until you have the cash in hand to pay for it.

This philosophy might have worked for the author, but he has a one-person company. The primary distinction of an entrepreneurial venture over a small business is that the entrepreneurial venture has value the owner can extract upon exit. A one-person business is unlikely to have much value that can be sold, so his advice landed with a thud for this long-time entrepreneur.

As someone who has started, owned, run, and sold several high-growth businesses, I have plenty of experience with debt. We had as much as $19 million of it at our peak. And yes, debt can be bad, especially when you use it to acquire nonincome-producing assets that do nothing for you beyond increasing your overhead. It is also bad if you don't have the income to pay it off.

Even with as much debt as we had, however, we never defaulted on any of it, nor did we fail to make any payments on time. And we never could have done what we did and achieved the successes we had without that debt capital.

Imagine being in the real estate development business or property management business and not being able to use debt. Some of the most profitable projects we ever did were ones where we financed most of our investment in the property. If you can do that and then either sell the project at a profit or operate it on a positive cash flow basis while you pay down the debt and at the same time have an asset that is increasing in value, you have a home run.

Debt doesn't work just for real estate businesses. It is also very helpful for a professional service business that has to perform work, bill clients, and then collect their money, sometimes months later. Being able to finance that is crucial to your ability to hire the people you need and keep them on the payroll until they start paying for themselves.

In other words, debt has its place, especially if you consider the alternatives of not growing the business at all or only using equity capital to fuel growth.

Equity capital, which means selling a piece of your business to someone, is far from the panacea it is often painted to be. Entrepreneurship programs in some colleges of business measure the amount of funding their students' new ventures raise and report on that as a measure of success. But while it may be impressive that someone is willing to put cash into your idea, it may not be the best thing for you or your business. In fact, if possible, I would encourage you not to pursue outside equity if there is any way to avoid it.

Here are some reasons why:

Outside equity investors bring outside influence. When you sell equity to someone, they are going to want a say in how the business is run (rightfully so!).

Most will want a seat on your board. They might want approval rights over any major expenditures or what you can pay yourself. They might insist on veto rights over any decision. And most will check in with you frequently and question your every decision. This can be a problem if they don't have the same understanding of your business or market that you do.

The entire business strategy and plan may have to change to accommodate the investor's thinking—especially if getting them out means paying them back for their equity with cash that you have already deployed.

You will be working for someone else. No one starts a business because they want to work for someone else and live another person's dream. But that is exactly what happens to many entrepreneurs who get outside equity capital. So why take someone else's money, which in effect makes them your boss? You aren't going to be happy. And in extreme cases, return-driven investors can fire the founders from the very companies they created.

I'm convinced there are some people out there—particularly those with certain technology-based ventures—who don't really want to be self-employed. If they can get enough grants and outside equity contributions, they can get a paycheck from the business. There's always a chance they hit it big and can maintain a small part of their equity and get a payout at some point, and I guess this is their lower-risk version of success.

But then I have to think they will be less motivated because they have less control and less to gain from the business' success. That isn't a good recipe for long-term success in my mind. And as I like to say, if you always think long-term, before you know it, the future is here and all those investments will pay off.

Equity investors in start-ups have huge expectations for their returns. Think about it from their perspective. Most new businesses fail, which means they will lose their investment. To make up for those losses, they have to bake in extraordinary returns on the ones that do make it. That could be anywhere from ten to fifty times their original investment over a three- to five-year period.

This is expressed as a "50X return" when you hear the jargon flying. Ten to fifty times their original investment is a huge number. The only way they can get that much is if you are very successful and then sell the business at the end of their investment period. You have to ask yourself if you are creating this business and working to make it successful just to have it sold out from under you?

It can create bad habits. Too much investment on the front-end allows the firm to be less disciplined about how it spends money. That lack of discipline can turn into a lack of success over the long haul. Undercapitalized companies can fare better over time because they have to be more thoughtful about how they use every dollar.

Equity can be very expensive capital. If you accept the premise that business value is directly linked to the revenue it is able to generate, as the business grows, so does the value. One of our businesses consistently generated a 50 percent-plus annual return on equity (not including owner salaries and benefits!) over a thirteen-year period. Someone who invested $15,000 had an asset worth $120,000 five or six years later. We had to pay that money back to them when they exited.

Compare that to the cost of debt. The business line of credit we recently renewed in one of our companies has a 4.75 percent interest rate. That is less than a tenth of what the annual cost of equity would have been.

Entrepreneurs often seek equity versus debt because, in most cases, the equity doesn't have to be paid back if the business fails. But if the business succeeds, you will pay dearly for that equity capital.

I wish more founders would fight the urge to bring in outside equity and instead focus on minimizing their start-up capital requirements through a wide range of bootstrapping tactics and strategies such as MVP (minimum viable product) so they can get their product or service out in the market with some sales and then refine it over time.

The bottom line is this. Many times (not always), debt is necessary and beneficial to the business. Borrow any money that you can, and then when things start to take off, bring in more equity capital through selling stock to key employees. These people will be the most motivated to make the thing successful. They also will make the transition easier when you exit the business because they are owner/managers who actually understand how to run the business.

Business owners who refuse to take on any debt will probably either not be able to grow their business or have to bring in outside equity investors. As a friend of mine said to me the other day, "Debt may have strings attached, but equity has chains!"

10

Avoiding Blunders in Your Business Plan

N ow that you've done all the prework to ensure you are ready to launch a business, you need to take the next big step of putting your ideas in writing.

The exercise of putting together a business plan—a good business plan—will help you identify gaps you might have missed, set targets to focus on as a business, and, of course, share your vision with others.

I have seen so many business plans for new ventures it would make your head spin. I don't think it would be an overstatement if I said I had seen a thousand or more. Some of them were fantastic, grabbed your attention right off the bat, and made you think, "Wow—these people must be geniuses!" Others were ho-hum and made you think, "These people won't make it a week."

If you are creating a business plan and want to be in the "must be geniuses" category, here are some of the things you should do to avoid the deficiencies I've seen in so many of the "won't make it a week" plans:

1. Quickly and clearly describe what the business does.

I always put this as number one because it needs to be at the beginning of the plan. It may seem obvious, but believe me—many times, I read and read and reread and still can't figure out what the business actually does. This is especially true for technology companies. Avoid buzzwords and jargon, and spell it out in terms a twelve-year-old would get.

This is super important!

2. Clearly explain how the business makes money.

Here's another one you would think would be obvious but isn't: How does the business make money? It's one thing to have an idea to fill a need, but it's another to turn that into a business that has a clear revenue model

An Incoherent Plan

I once was asked to coach the founders of a start-up from our technology park. They were seeking a National Science Foundation grant, and my job was to help them with their business plan so they could get the money—something on the order of $500,000.

Unfortunately, their plan wasn't just weak, it was absolutely incoherent. There were so many buzzwords and acronyms in it that I couldn't begin to understand what they did, much less how they were going to make money on it.

I called the CEO several times to gain clarity, and he never called me back. I don't think he liked that I didn't understand his business. But the people he was trying to get capital from were probably going to be more like me than him—not knowledgeable about his specific technology.

Despite my calls and subsequent emails, I was never able to reach the guy and help fix his plan, and to my knowledge, they didn't get the grant money they were seeking.

and that can explain the costs of doing what you will do versus the revenue you will receive for doing it.

The bigger the spread between cost and revenue, the better.

3. Clearly describe the market.

The best business is one that serves a tightly defined market that is huge, and the business only needs a small fraction of it to be profitable. Determining the market and its size takes some thought and research, but it's crucial information, and you cannot ignore it.

4. Clearly describe the target clients or customers.

Every aspect of the business needs to be designed around the targeted clients or customers, so they need to be clearly identified and described. An understanding of the customer's wants and needs should be clear in every aspect of your marketing, advertising, promotions, and product or service offerings. It should factor into decisions about your facilities and the employees you hire. It should be embedded in every aspect of the business.

One tactic I have suggested many times over the years is to do something called a "target customer collage." This is where you show pictures of your ideal customer(s) along with everything they like to do, eat, watch, listen to, where they live, and so on. Having a very clear picture in mind of who the business serves is always helpful to a new business.

5. Provide testimonials from target clients or customers.

Throwing in a bunch of quotes from the kinds of clients or customers you plan on targeting adds credibility to your plan. There's little better than a specific (and maybe even well-recognized) target customer saying something to the effect of, "If this product or service was available, I would buy it!"

6. Include clear expectations for investors.

If you are trying to attract equity investors, they will want to know exactly what they can expect from their involvement—the offering along with exit options and an estimate of the business's value if the financial targets are met.

What will they get for the money they invest? What are the buyback terms? What rights do they have?

They will justifiably want your input on what that value could be for the business at some point down the road when you or they exit.

Investors, and everyone else who looks at a business plan, wants to know what the break-even volume is and how long it will take you to get there. The lower the number and the faster it looks like it will come, the better!

They also will want to know that you are willing to take some personal financial risks to help the venture succeed. I have recently seen two cases of new ventures that probably could have borrowed the operating capital they needed based on certain assets that could be financed with bank loans, but the owners were seeking equity instead because they would not personally guarantee the debt.

It's a huge red flag for investors when the founders have so little faith that they won't make the commitment it takes to sign up for debt. Same thing when it comes to contributing cash as a founder.

No skin in the game is not a good sign. Be willing to make that commitment if you really want to start this thing.

7. Provide the right information on the founders.

Investors or lenders care far more about the people running the business than they do the business itself. If they have confidence that you have the right background, character, and orientation to succeed, they will be more likely to give you what you want from them. Spell it out. And spell out the exact roles everyone will be filling, as well. (Side note: Do not propose co-CEOs for your business. It rarely works.)

8. Identify your outside directors or advisory board.

This is especially crucial if you are young or relatively inexperienced in the industry you will be serving. The right outside directors or advisers can instantly bring credibility to the plan and reduce the perceived risk of getting involved with you. And believe me, many entrepreneurs are shocked to find out how willing some very experienced people are to help as directors or advisers—in many cases for little to no compensation. (See chapter 7.)

9. Have financial projections that make sense.

Realistic income statements, balance sheets, and cash flow projections are the heart of the business plan, and they have to add up.

Why would a $10 million annual revenue plan require $9 million in cash in the bank for working capital? Why don't income statements and balance sheets tie together? Why is seasonality not considered in the forecasts? Why is there a line for taxes on the income statement of an S-corp? Why wasn't the negative cash flow accounted for in the starting capital requirements?

These types of financial projections are critical in the plan, and they have to be done right.

10. Correctly estimate the marketing budget.

Marketing activities and costs are almost always underestimated in the start-up plans I see. I typically ask something like, "Why do you think you will have this hockey stick–like revenue growth while spending a tenth of what established companies in this industry are spending?" It makes no sense. You probably need to spend two or three times the industry norms, especially when starting out. And in some cases, the marketing activities have to start well before the official launch of the business. That needs to be noted and accounted for.

Some of these ten "dos" might seem obvious, but I wouldn't point them out if they weren't so commonly absent from the business plans of start-up founders. Rather than tempting fate and seeing if you can overcome such blunders, take my advice and avoid them.

11

The Biggest Mistakes Company Founders Make

I quoted some statistics way back in the introduction that are worth repeating before we go any further: Approximately 20 percent of small businesses fail within the first year, and 70 percent don't last more than a decade.[1]

Outside forces—the economy, a pandemic, a natural disaster in some faraway country—typically get the blame. But as a student of business for most of my life, I can tell you that many businesses don't achieve their potential—and some don't make it all—simply because of mistakes the founders made, many of which could have been avoided.

I've already covered several of those mistakes, but some, like those daunting statistics, are worth repeating before we close out this section of the book and move into topics that involve leading and managing a business. So here are some of the most common mistakes I've seen founders make:

Hiring friends and family. Again, I touched on this in previous chapters, but it bears repeating. The inevitable breakdown occurs when people who are not qualified and have personal relationships with the founder are unable to perform their jobs, and it compromises virtually everything the business is trying to accomplish. Then you have the additional problem that hiring relatives causes with the rest of your employees when the perception is that they were hired more for their bloodlines than their skill sets.

Immediately looking for equity capital. Why give away your business before you have even started it? I really think the popular media has

---

1. Jimmy O'Donnell, Daniel Newman, and Kenan Fikri, "The Startup Surge? Unpacking 2020 Trends in Business Formation," Economic Innovation Group, February 8, 2021, https://eig.org/the-startup-surge-business-formation-trends -in-2020/#.

promoted this notion that once you've got your idea for a business, the next thing you are supposed to do is look for capital. It isn't!

The next thing you really need is a good business plan—one that minimizes the amount of capital required to get the business going and prove its viability. With the right business idea and the right plan, you may not need any outside capital.

Getting equity capital from people who don't understand your business or industry. If the investors are purely financially driven, they won't share your passion for the business and probably won't see the opportunity for what you are proposing as clearly as you do. This could mean they will want you to do things that aren't in the best interests of your business over the long haul.

People who understand your business and industry, however, may be able to provide real help and insight. They may also have all manner of connections that could help your business succeed—including possible clients and/or customers, sources of supply, and valuable connections with regulators or government authorities that could be pivotal.

For example, I recently had a client who was approached with a potential private equity deal. While the valuation was impressive, the best aspect of the potential deal was that the guy heading the fund came out of the very same industry and specialty of their business. The odds of long-term success are so much better in a scenario like this.

Using precious capital to buy assets that could have been financed. I always like to use the example of two individuals I knew who started an electrical contracting business. They had $27,000 between them, which should have been adequate starting capital for what they were trying to do. The first thing they did was buy a new truck and pay cash for it—$25,000 at the time— which then meant they had no money to do things such as pay for the materials they needed to do a job. It resulted in their failure within a year.

Making big, fixed overhead commitments before there is any sense of how the business will do. This, too, is so common. The overly expensive retail space, too much office space, or worse—buying a building right out of the gate when there is absolutely no idea what demand will be and how much or how little space will be needed. The same applies to hiring too-expensive people too early in your development.

Farm out everything you can to keep costs low and fixed commitments to a minimum!

Vastly underestimating the marketing and promotions budget. I see this more often than not. Founders who cannot see that tackling huge problems where the whole world is a potential customer takes a tremendous amount of marketing and promotional dollars to get any traction in the market. So they don't spend it—and don't get it, either.

Not testing the product or service adequately with consumers. I suffered from this one myself with a business that I cofounded with two partners. Our majority owner and inventor of our products thought he knew better than the customers we were targeting on what their needs were. He refused to have focus groups made up of target customers. As a result, one of our products completely missed the mark because our customers did not like certain aspects of it. I suspected we would have some problems there, but his unwillingness to consider customer input was a big part of our eventual downfall.

Not forming a board of advisers who can help the business get off the ground. The board of advisers is one of the most affordable and best ways to get effective mentoring and sound advice if you pick the right people—those from your industry, those who have been in the same business, those who work in potential client or customer organizations, and those who have experience you can benefit from are the best candidates. Many will work for free or for a few thousand dollars a meeting. This could be a bargain if you get successful people in their fields.

Not getting a partner who complements you. Many founders end up as partners with someone who is just like them. That is a huge mistake and will undoubtedly lead to role conflict and possibly relationship problems—while at the same time ensuring that certain skill or orientation deficiencies when you have very little to spend on talent don't get addressed.

Not good!

The best partners in my experience are those with similar values but completely different backgrounds and skills. They share a dogged determination to succeed in spite of obstacles. They have respect for each other and what each brings to the business, and they are able to work out their differences. Then they each have a more natural role that is less likely to result in conflict. Conflict among founders is not usually productive! In fact, conflict between founding partners is a common cause of business failure.

Taking too much money out too soon. The business is the goose that has the potential to lay golden eggs. If you ever want to see those "golden eggs," taking care of the goose is your number one priority. It needs all the care and feeding you can give it. If you starve it or don't keep the heat on, or worse yet, eat it, you will never see a golden egg. Don't take too much cash out of the business because your personal wants and needs are too high.

So, how do you take care of that goose, especially when it's still a gosling? That's the subject of part 2.

PART II

Into the Great Unknown

It's one thing to endlessly talk and fantasize about starting a business, but many would-be entrepreneurs end up like the fictional Walter Mitty and never go beyond the daydreamer stage. So how do you actually get started and go from a coffee shop wantrepreneur to someone who's actually earning a living from a business you've created?

If you read part 1, you have a good idea of things you need to consider and do before you start your business, so hopefully that will give you the confidence you need to make the leap. Once you leap into the great unknown, you'll want to gain and keep the momentum that leads to success.

12

Getting Your New Business off the Ground

Preparation precedes action, but action must follow preparation. So here are a few ways to prepare and act on your entrepreneurial dreams now that it's time to put up or shut up and step into the great unknown.

Minimize your personal overhead and stockpile your resources. When you launch your business, you want to be in a position where every single dollar that will benefit the business stays in the business. So, in addition to keeping your personal overhead as low as possible, you'll want to stockpile everything that might help you get by with little to no money. Once your personal overhead is low and you feel you can get by for a while on very little (I would say one to three years), you will be more likely to actually start your business.

Living on Less

When I started Mark Zweig & Associates in 1988, I was dead broke. I had just lost my job. I had relocated from Texas to Massachusetts only six-and-a-half months earlier. We had a one-year-old baby. And my then-wife was not working (nor licensed to work in the Commonwealth of Massachusetts). We also had just bought an old house with 5 percent down and gutted half of it in anticipation of a major renovation.

My new business quickly secured contracts worth about $8,500 a month—about what I was earning in my previous job. However, we decided to live on $2,000 a month and reinvest most of the rest into our business. We did this for several years, and it was pivotal to making the business healthy and sustainable because it allowed us to staff up and rent more office space, which, in turn, led to earning much more than $8,500 a month.

Share your business plan. Everyone likes their ideas to be heard, so give your employees a chance to provide input on the business plan. You don't have to use every idea, but you might be surprised at how many good ones come from those who will work with you.

When you share the plan with others, including employees you add along the way, they are more likely to do what's needed to help you succeed because they know why you are in business, what you are trying to become, what your goals are, what rules you follow, and what you do that makes your business successful.

Surround yourself with encouragers. There is a big difference between people who tell you what you want to hear and those who are supportive and encouraging but urge caution and diligence before starting a new business. You want to surround yourself with the latter, if possible.

As for those who are completely negative and only discourage you, spend too much time with people like that, and you will never take the plunge.

Oftentimes, people who never had a business or didn't grow up in a business-owning family may think that any venture is too risky, and so, with the best of intentions, they will discourage you from taking the leap. You don't have to ditch them as friends, but you don't have to listen to them, either. Expand your social network to include people who encourage you to start your business, and you will be more likely to do it.

Break down the process. Starting a business from scratch can seem overwhelming, so break it down into thirty, fifty, or a hundred small steps. Taking those steps, one at a time, helps build the momentum you need to see it through.

In part 1, I covered the steps that come prior to starting the business—things like getting input from others on your business idea and writing a good business plan. As you move forward, your to-do list will include things like filing the required paperwork for whatever legal form your business requires (LLC, S-corp, C-corp, etc.) and opening a bank account—pretty much everything that must be done to implement the plan you created.

This applies beyond starting a business, by the way. Breaking a problem down into many small tasks is a technique used by many people who accomplish great things. Try it, and see if it helps get you off the starting line.

Test your concept. Once you actually have a client or customer who is willing to buy, you will likely have more confidence that you can start your business. The whole idea of creating a minimum viable product is to validate your idea and get the thing going. Sure, it won't be perfect at first, but you will refine your offerings and business plan over time—and meanwhile, there will be some revenue coming in and a chance to get real customer feedback.

When people do this and prove their concept, they will be more likely to keep it all going and actually make the commitment to launch the business.

Constantly look for new talent. Keep an eye out for employees and independent contractors who would add value to your team before you need them and before you can afford to add them.

Finding people with skills you don't have so that you can put their skills to use when you need them is one of the most important things you can do. If you don't build your network in advance of the need, you could be forced to go it alone and miss a chance to grow, or you could bring the wrong person onto your team because you are under pressure.

I am constantly on the lookout for anyone who is hard-working, intelligent, nice, and has good communication skills—regardless of their educational or experience background, I will try to find a way to create a job around them.

My first CFO for Mark Zweig & Associates used to clean my house. Prior to cleaning houses, she was the number two financial person in a service company with more than a thousand employees. Another fellow who worked for us for more than twenty years was a financial guy who was working as a telemarketer. We met one day in the hallway of our office building, and it wasn't long before he joined our team. You never know someone's real story or their real capabilities until you get to know them!

Build your client/customer database. Email marketing works for both business-to-consumer and business-to-business businesses. Don't let anyone tell you otherwise. So, you need a good email list. The best way to start is with your personal contact directory, then add the email addresses of anyone who inquires about or buys from you, and look for things of value you can give away in exchange for an email address. You also can build your list from trade shows and professional or trade groups.

Your client or customer management database should be conveniently available to every employee so that they can maintain it on a daily basis. It has to work on a smartphone as well as a regular computer. They should also be able to quickly see the buying history of anyone they are dealing with to help them better understand the value of the customer and better serve them.

One of the most critical things we did with Mark Zweig & Associates/Zweig White/Zweig Group was to have one database on every employee's desk that housed every single project, purchase, seminar registration, inquiry, and so on. When we sold that business in 2004, we had data on more than two hundred thousand clients and customers that included every single thing we had ever sold them or tried to sell them. It made our business very valuable to a buyer that had other products and services to sell to our same client base.

Market and promote aggressively. Make sure to budget (and spend) more than enough for marketing and promotion. This is a huge weakness for most businesses, especially new businesses. Entrepreneurs are often so in love with their concept that they think everyone else automatically will feel the same way. As a result, they spend very little (or nothing at all) on promotional activities and end up wondering why customers aren't flocking to their doors.

Most new businesses need to spend two or three times what their competitors spend on promotion just to get some momentum. The exact percentage of revenue varies widely based on the type of business. But this I do know—if most companies in your business spend 4 percent of revenue on marketing, you may find that 8 percent or even 12 percent of revenue brings you more revenue, creates faster growth, allows you to charge more, and gives you better profitability than your competition.

At Mark Zweig & Associates/Zweig White, we spent an average of more than 14 percent of revenues on promotion each year, which I am certain was at least twice what our primary competitors were spending. It allowed us to grow faster, be more profitable, provide better opportunities for our people, and be more valuable at the time of exit.

It's also important to relentlessly protect the brand you market. I see so many businesses with multiple names, unreadable logos, bad or no signage, and inconsistent use of colors. All of this is avoidable. Simple repetition of something that is immediately recognizable as coming from your company is crucial. I'm also big on vehicle wraps, darker backgrounds for signage (as opposed to white), and worker uniforms or shirts, and getting all of this out on every social media channel available to you.

Be flexible and open to change. The market might not respond the way you want it to, so you must be ready to change direction. Things rarely, if ever, go according to plan. Pay attention to what is going on in the world, your industry, and with your clients or customers, and see what is selling and what's not so you can make changes if needed.

For instance, if things aren't going well, you need to discern whether you have ineffective marketing or product or service offerings that the market just doesn't want. I have been in this position with my own businesses more than once. If you are trying to sell something no one wants, you may need to dump that offering, and that's not easy if you are the type who doesn't give up easily.

You also need the wisdom to know when chasing certain market trends will cost you more business than it brings in. This is the dark side of listening too closely to the market because there are times you might end up throwing out your primary customers to get new ones. Cadillac, for instance, decided to go after younger buyers, but in the process, they lost many of their older customers who were accustomed to rolling couches. The jury is still out as to if their strategy will work.

Sometimes you have to change the business model entirely if the market is telling you to do so. If you are too inflexible and invested in your original ideas, you may not be able to adapt to the market quickly enough. But if you are willing to change and be smart about when and how to adjust, you are more likely to turn challenges into opportunities. For example, Zweig Group responded to the COVID-19 pandemic in 2020 by creating a whole slate of online training programs and a first-ever online conference that drew nearly two thousand participants. This was critical to its ability to emerge stronger postpandemic than it was prior to it.

Know your cash flow. Your business will live or die based on its cash flow, so it's critical to create and continuously revise your cash-flow forecasts. Know your break-even and exactly what you need to bring in every month or even every day to not fall behind. Schedule all payments and estimate receipts on a spreadsheet. Revise your forecast daily. And share these reports with your employees, so they know what's going on.

Look ahead as many months as you can. I like to look at least eight weeks—with a week-by-week view of what we think we will bring in versus what we know will go out. This exercise will tell you whether or not you are likely to have the cash you need to meet your obligations. If a shortage looms ahead, you will have some time to deal with it before it hits. Get advance payments. Slow up on disbursements. Make new sales. Negotiate terms with vendors. There is always something you can do.

Truthfully, having the discipline to do this was essential to any successes I ever had, and it allowed me to keep ownership inside my businesses rather than going to the outside for equity partners who may have had entirely different ideas about how we should do business.

Listen and respond to feedback. If you are the founder or owner of the enterprise, don't cut yourself off from inquiries and complaints. This information is way too critical for your business.

Be sure that all inquiries and customer service complaints come directly to you. And when you get one, respond immediately. If you don't have time to respond now, what makes you think you will later?

I will never forget how Jay Steinfeld, CEO of Blinds.com, a $200 million company at the time, responded to a minor complaint I had about their product that I submitted late on a Friday afternoon. Within ten minutes, I heard back from him personally. He wasn't too busy to deal with me—a customer.

We struck up a conversation later that night (a Friday, mind you!) that showed me how in-tune he was with his customers and company and led me to have him as a speaker at our annual Hot Firm and A/E Industry Awards Conference.

Clients, customers, suppliers, and employees love it when you give them an immediate reaction to whatever their question, concern, or idea is—even if all you say is, "I don't know but will get back to you shortly."

This type of responsiveness from the founder sets a great example for everyone else in the company to do the same, and making it part of your culture speeds up everything you do.

Have a monthly bonus program that includes all employees. The way I like to handle bonuses is purely mathematically. I'm not a fan of subjective bonus distributions, which is the way many business owners handle things.

I like to decide at the beginning of each year how much of the cash basis profits will be paid to all employees and then tie this bonus pool to the open-book report. That way, if the company makes a $100,000 cash profit for the month, a certain percentage of that will go out to all.

Most of the time, we set this number for the year between 15 and 25 percent of cash profits. Any months where there is a cash basis loss would have to be made up in the months to follow before any bonus monies are paid out.

In general, I have four strategies for rewarding people:

1. Divide the employee group into two major pots—those who could have a business of their own and those who don't have such options. Some people (those who could make it on their own) give up a lot when they take a job with a company, and that is always at the forefront of my mind when I consider how to pay them. Those who could have their own businesses are going to do better—a lot better—than those who don't have that option. These employees share another portion of the pie on top of the all-employee pool, which they also participate in.

2. Pay bonuses based on firm or unit performance rather than individual performances. I am not a big fan of most so-called incentive compensation plans. They are too often a poor substitute for management doing its job—that is, reforming or weeding out nonperformers. Such incentive plans are supposed to get a message across to low performers to shape up or ship out. Yet rarely do they leave—they are poor performers, after all, and have few options. Plus, there is the inescapable fact that little of what most businesses do is an individual effort.

3. Paying extra for performance is not as critical as *not* paying for poor performance. If you want morale to go up and total labor costs to go down, get rid of the deadbeats on your staff. You don't need to go crazy paying extra for great performance.

4. Tracking and reporting performance may be more important than paying extra for it. People like a scorecard, whether they get paid to perform or not. It's reinforcing. Sometimes the game is more important than the prize.

Add new products and services. There are two things I am sure of that help a business keep growing. One is to keep trying new marketing and advertising approaches. The other is to keep bringing out more product and service offerings. This keeps your customer base interested and gives you more opportunities to demonstrate how good it is to do business with you.

Each of these new offerings is a point of entry for you to develop a new client or customer. Some may prove to be unprofitable or not lead to additional sales. Those can be cut and new offerings tried out.

13

The Importance of Proper Pricing

When you look at successful privately held businesses—the ones that really make it and survive (and thrive) for years—a common theme emerges: They aren't giving away whatever it is they're selling.

Pricing is crucial to success, yet it rarely gets the attention or scrutiny it deserves. And undercharging is one of the most common mistakes start-up founders make. They think (erroneously) that being the cheapest will get them the business they need to grow and prosper. It may help make some sales, but the lack of margin (the difference between the cost of what you are selling and the price that you are selling it for) will kill a business quickly.

A new small business is almost always better off with a high price, low volume strategy. I have used it in every business I was a part of and can tell you it is essential.

Let's face it, you are going to have low volume. You are a new business. No one knows who you are yet. You are probably undercapitalized. You cannot compete with the economies of scale that a larger, more established business has.

What choice do you have if you want to make any money? The one sure way you can beat the bigger companies is to provide better quality or service. And the only way you can do that is to charge more than they do.

Let's say you are in the business of selling tacos. You can sell a three-taco meal for $6 to undercut all of your competitors, or you can sell a three-taco meal for $9. If your cost for food and labor to provide three tacos is $4.50, then you need to sell three times as many taco meals at $6 to make what you'd make selling them for $9.

You might think you can sell three meals at the lower price easier than one at the higher price and thereby make your margin. But there are other implications of the low-price, higher-volume approach. The customer experience, for instance, will be different. The lines will be longer, and the employees will be more stressed to keep the food coming out and the restaurant clean. The facility also might prove inadequate, requiring a greater investment in fixed costs.

Additional challenges can result from a low-price strategy if your business sells services to other businesses. Managers or business developers in these organizations often are the ones quoting whatever services the company sells, and, without proper pricing oversight, they will tend to give the work away.

Why? First, they know management favors those people who can sell the work. Second, it's easier to sell anything when the prices are too low. It's not hard to trade a dollar for eighty-five cents.

There are long-term ramifications of letting this happen—most of all that it's hard to raise your prices in the future. That problem is compounded when you work in a close-knit industry where competitors may talk and compare. The result is that the business may never recover from a history of prices that started out too low.

If you want to charge higher prices, of course, clients and customers must see sufficient value in what you are selling. That takes one or both of the following: First, you should have a better product or service than your competition. Second, you must convince buyers of the benefits of buying from your organization over doing business with a competitor.

To have a better product or service usually means you must have a better design, better materials, better equipment, and better people. And to convince a sufficient number of potential buyers of your benefits, you usually must spend more on marketing. Both of these things—high-quality products and services and better and more marketing—cost money. Both will also drive volume and create more value in the enterprise, with value creation being one of the primary goals of ownership.

My experience is that when you get into this virtuous cycle, the value created will greatly exceed the cost to create it.

14

Opening Up Your Books

O pen-book management—sharing key financial information and other company performance metrics with everyone in the organization—is a tool any business owner can use to their advantage, and it's best to begin using it as early in your journey as possible.

It was a key part of our management approach at Zweig Group from the beginning nearly thirty-four years ago, and we also helped implement it in some form in dozens of client companies over the years.

Yet very few entrepreneurs and small business owners practice it, and they'll give all kinds of reasons why.

"Our people wouldn't understand the numbers if we shared them."

My response: Your people are smarter than you think and will understand it if you educate them.

"Our employees will be upset if they see how much money we are making."

My response: You need to educate your people on why making a profit is essential and where that money goes. And if you are embarrassed by how much your business makes relative to how much of that bounty you share with your people, maybe you are being greedy. Not to mention, studies have shown that employees who are not informed about their firm's performance are generally under the impression that owners make much more than they actually do from their businesses.[1,2]

"People will be upset if they see what other people make."

---

1. Don Harkey, "Is It Time for Open-Book Management?," People Centric Consulting Group, January 3, 2020, https://blog.peoplecentric.com/blog/is-it-time-for-open-book-management.

2. Mark J. Perry, "The General Public Thinks the Average Company Makes a 36% Profit Margin, Which Is about 5X Too High, Part II," AEI, January 15, 2018, https://www.aei.org/carpe-diem/the-public-thinks-the-average-company-makes-a-36-profit-margin-which-is-about-5x-too-high-part-ii/.

My response: Never share what individual salaries and bonuses are. Individuals could feel they are paid fairly until they find out someone else in the same or similar role makes $2,000 a year more than they do. That is not part of open-book management.

"Our employees will be scared if they see what poor condition we're in."

My response: Some may, but odds are, they will think things are even worse than they really are if you haven't told them the situations. It's your job as the owner to keep everyone informed and educated!

"We don't have good numbers and can't get them out quickly enough."

My response: You need good numbers for yourself, so you better fix that situation quickly.

"We don't want our competitors to see our numbers."

My response: Why? What are the real odds they will see it, and more importantly, what would they do with that information if they had it?

In my experience, none of these excuses are legitimate, and business owners are missing out on the wide variety of benefits they could get from using open-book management. Here are a few:

- Open-book management can help train employees in how your business makes money, which hopefully will make your business more successful while building bench strength for future management roles.
- Open-book management helps build trust between management and employees. Employees appreciate that they are being clued in as to how the business is really performing.
- Open-book management helps the owner(s) prepare the firm for the owner(s) eventual exit because there are other people who have been prepared to step in in their absence.
- Open-book management creates accountability and can help generate peer pressure to perform. All of the numbers are out in the open for everyone to see.
- Open-book management forces management to have timely and accurate reporting because everyone expects to see the report on a consistent basis.
- Open-book management reports can be used to keep the firm's lenders and investors informed on how the business is doing.

- Open-book management should be motivational to all employees. It helps contribute to psychological ownership. This alone should be enough to implement it.

According to a 2017 article in *Forbes* magazine by Bill Fotsch and John Case, "companies register as much as a 30% increase in productivity and profitability in the first year alone when they implement the (open book) approach properly."[3]

My response to that: Business owners, what are you waiting for?

---

3. Bill Fotsch and John Case, "The Business Case for Open-Book Management," *Forbes.com*, July 25, 2017, https://www.forbes.com/sites/fotschcase/2017/07/25 /the-business-case-for-open-book-management/?sh=76e0804a5883.

15

Your Family and Your Business

Most discussions about starting a company center on the various aspects of the actual business and the acumen you, as an entrepreneur, need to give the business the best opportunities for success. And rightly so. What's often ignored, however, is your family and its influence on your entrepreneurial venture.

Here's the truth—if your family isn't behind you, you will have problems.

In chapters 19 and 20, I'll write more about maintaining the right priorities and finding a healthy balance between work and the rest of life, all of which connect to your family relationships. But for now, as you launch your new business, make sure you are aware of, dealing with, and preparing for the potential issues you may face related to your family.

For instance, if you need to borrow money from a bank and you don't have a long history of successful operations along with a very healthy balance sheet, not only will you be asked to personally guarantee the debt, but your spouse will also be required by the bank to sign.

Your spouse may not know this is normal. And as the numbers get really big (say millions of dollars), it may seem overly risky to them. That could pose a problem for you!

Engage in transparent conversations with your spouse where you share not only the regulatory requirements but also the reasons why the business needs the money and the plan for paying it back. Different spouses will desire different levels of detail. Some may want to go to meetings with you when you talk with bankers or your accountant, for instance. Some might want visibility into the business's bookkeeping. Others will just want a high-level overview.

Starting a new venture also will have a significant impact on your family's budget. When families are accustomed to a certain income from your employment, it can be hard for them to understand if you aren't bringing home what you used to make in that job—at least for the first year or two or at other times in the growth and development of your company.

The sooner you begin educating your spouse and children about why these short-term sacrifices are necessary to achieve your family's longer-term goals, the more understanding they will be and the better you can all prepare for the changes you might need to make when it comes to your expectations about your standard of living.

And as your income goes down (temporarily, you hope), the commitments on your time away from your family go up. The hours required from the owners of a fledgling business or a growth business can cause friction with spouses and children. The business, at times, might require travel or work on weekends or evenings, making it impossible for you to fulfill other family responsibilities that your spouse or children (rightfully) expect of you. They may not understand why you can't be at every soccer game or why you have to be on the phone when it's time to read to the kids and put them to bed.

I can't tell you how many times I got in trouble with my then-spouse because I was on my phone at night or while on vacation. She came from a family background where both of her parents were teachers who didn't work like that, and it was hard for her to understand why I did. Your spouse may get the idea you love your business more than them—not a recipe for a happy relationship between two people!

This is a common problem, and you need to be empathetic while at the same time resolute in your need for help so you can do whatever the business requires from you. It will take a lot of understanding and teamwork, along with an open acknowledgment and appreciation from you for those who fill in for you when you need it most. That is going to take a lot of time, talk, and patience from you and your spouse.

Your spouse, kids, and even your parents also may not appreciate the daily stress that comes with starting a business and having payroll obligations you have to meet—not to mention people problems, problems collecting money, regulatory problems, customer service problems, and so on.

If they don't have that appreciation, you won't get the emotional support you may need at times. If you don't get it from them, who will you get it from? This is a serious problem! It may require you to restrict your work activities to only so much time at night or to certain times when you are not at work so as to have some work-life balance.

An additional dynamic is added to the mix when your spouse and children work in the business.

As I previously mentioned, it's generally not such a great idea to hire family members, especially in businesses that employ a lot of smart, educated people. Employees will assume a child is getting special treatment, even if they aren't. And if you feel the pressure to avoid special treatment, you may swing too far in the other direction and end up holding back your child—the last thing you want to do by employing them.

If you do plan to hire your children, my advice is to never hire them directly into management. Work them through low-level jobs in various areas. Encourage them to work somewhere else before coming into your business. Treat them fairly, like you would any other employee. Don't over-promote them, and don't artificially hold them back. And get your spouse on board with what you are trying to do so that they understand the complexities of nepotism.

And what if your spouse works with you in the business? That's not uncommon, but it's also risky. I have seen businesses destroy marriages, especially when the couple works together. If you and your spouse are working co-owners, make sure you have well-defined, nonoverlapping roles. The last thing you want is to comanage the business as a two-headed monster. Your employees will be confused, and you will have conflict in

Relational Brilliance

David and Bonnie Penzias founded Wellesley Information Services in 1991, grew it into a successful business, and sold it in 2011. They are two brilliant people. They both earned electrical engineering degrees from the University of Pennsylvania, and Bonnie earned a master's in computer science from Harvard while he picked up an MBA from Penn's Wharton School.

Not only were they smart when it came to business and technology, but they were also smart about how they worked together. They drove separate cars to work, for instance, and had offices in far corners of their building. They also had completely distinct roles in their business and tried not to talk about work at home. It worked out really well for them, and they are still married.

your business and personal lives. Also, make sure you have time at home where you stay away from the business talk, or it could completely consume you.

When it comes to all of these issues that can involve your family, my advice is to take a proactive approach, especially when it comes to communicating what's going on and why. The more they know, the better. But you also need to be proactive when it comes to listening to their concerns and needs. If the new business is all about you and your needs, your family is likely to feel neglected (because they are being neglected), and that can lead to bitterness and dissension that can destroy a family.

16

Building Foundational Relationships

t doesn't matter whether you are an entry-level employee in a *Fortune 100* company or a middle-aged person who owns your own business; your ability to build and maintain relationships with other people will have a huge impact on your success. This is particularly important when you are launching a new venture because hard work never happens in isolation. You need the help of other people.

There are things you can do to build valuable relationships with your bosses, clients, customers, suppliers, regulators, teammates, and subordinates. If you do these things in manipulative ways, then you might have a heart issue. But if you genuinely care about other people, then my advice on building and strengthening relationships will not only serve your needs but serve your colleagues as well.

Get off to a good start. First impressions are everything. Your body language says a lot. Stand up straight. Look alive. Don't cross your arms or clench your fists. Do you have a firm handshake? Do you look directly at the person you are meeting? Do you use their name during the conversation or act as if you have already forgotten it? When they hand you a business card, do you take a moment to look at it? All of these things are critical to what the other person will think of you.

Show interest in the other person. The best way to do this is to ask questions about them. Everyone likes to talk about themselves. It has been proven that when you ask people to share the things that are important to them, they are more likely to have a favorable impression of you. Pay attention to what the other person is telling you so you can parrot it back in the future. That shows you have a real interest and not just an artificial one.

As Dale Carnegie advised in his classic book *How to Win Friends and Influence People*, "Ask questions the other person will enjoy answering" and "Be a good listener."

Be helpful. People like other people who are helpful to them, so look for and act on opportunities to ease the burdens of the people around you. Matt Lewis, who became a manager in his family's multiple car dealership businesses while in his mid-twenties, says this is the best way to win the allegiance of older, more senior employees. Go help them do something that makes their day or job better. Don't do their jobs for them; do things that make their work easier and more enjoyable.

Open up about yourself. Share some of your personal information when it's appropriate to do so. What are your interests? Your challenges? What are some funny things you aren't so good at? It always helps to be humble and self-deprecating if you want someone to like you. But steer clear of politics unless you have a very, very close relationship and you are 100 percent certain the other person feels the same way you do.

Be kind and grateful. Hold the door open. Volunteer your seat to the older person. Rescue the lost dog. Treat restaurant servers like the humans they are. Say "hi" to the building janitor everyone else ignores. Say "please" and "thank you." Good manners are always appreciated, whether at the table or in an email. People will notice.

Be humble and self-deprecating. One of the best ways to get someone to like you is to make fun of yourself. And a little humility goes a long way. No one likes a braggart. I have erred on this one in the past.

Be responsive. Return each phone call promptly and apologize for not taking it when they called. Respond to emails as soon as possible, even if it's to say you will get back to someone later. Then get back to them. That applies to employees, clients, customers, suppliers, and friends. Responsiveness shows that you care.

Be reliable. Don't be late or fail to keep appointments. Being on time and not missing appointments show respect for the other person. Constantly rescheduling because of one crisis or higher priority after another tells the other person they aren't necessary. That makes you less likable.

Be thoughtful. Bringing a coffee to a friend in the morning or cleaning up the mess in the company kitchen created by other people is nice. Buying a Christmas present for someone you don't need to is nice. Remembering birthdays or employment anniversaries is nice. All of these things show you can be thoughtful.

Do the extra. This is crucial when it comes to clients and customers. If someone is unhappy with their meal, give it to them for free. Wash their car when someone spends $1,000 at your repair shop. Do the extra research you didn't have to do as a part of that consulting project. Sew the button on the shirt a customer brought to you for cleaning. Wash the windows at the end of the exterior paint job you just did on someone's house. Throw in the extra ranch dressing at no charge with the large pizza to go. These things make people like you.

Pay your bills promptly. Nothing makes suppliers and service providers like you more than a prompt payment. No one likes having to chase people down who owe them money. The quicker you pay, the better service you will get because those people will like you.

Make an effort to stay in touch. Show that your interest isn't just transactional. Call, text, or email (not as good as a call) people when you don't want anything from them. Just check on them and see how they are doing. Be the one who initiates the contact when the other person is silent. Send the holiday card even if they don't send one to you. Be a good friend by showing you care even if the other person isn't reciprocating.

This is one of the most important things you can do! No one likes people who only contact them when they want something. Stay in touch over the long haul. I have relationships with clients today that started forty years ago because I have done this.

Entire books have been written about building relationships, but if you start with the things I've covered in this chapter, it will help you be more successful, no matter who you are or what you do for a living.

Dealing with Professional Service Providers

To get your new venture going and to set it up for growth, you will inevitably need to work with a wide array of outside professionals who are experts in areas that you are not.

Some, like accountants, are common to any new venture, while others might only come into play if you are in a certain phase of your business growth or if you are in a certain type of business. One of my ventures, for instance, involved speculative real estate investing, so I learned a great deal about dealing with the various professional service providers that are involved with doing house renovations.

If you are involved in real estate development, the advisors I'm highlighting in this chapter are particularly critical. Regardless of your industry, remember that specialization rules and that you will need the help of qualified professionals.

Real estate agents. If your business involves buying, selling, or renting property, you will want to find and work with the most successful real estate agent in your area. Don't get a part-time hobbyist agent who is already a friend or someone you just happen to meet at an open house. You want someone who has proven over time that they can sell real estate. Where I live (Northwest Arkansas), that means someone who is selling at least $10 million to $20 million a year.

This person will have better connections, do a better job marketing your property, be a better negotiator on your behalf, and, most importantly, anticipate problems that could crop up in closing a sale. And when you show loyalty to them by never cutting them out of a sale, you will engender loyalty from them. All the good deals they discover (and if they are very successful, they will come up with deals) will go to you first.

This may be one of the most critical relationships you have in this type of business. I have worked with my agent, for instance, for sixteen years.

He has his own firm, is an attorney, and he also teaches real estate courses nationally. He has functioned as a true partner over the years, even though he never had any ownership in our business or projects. We would never have been as successful as we were in this business without his involvement.

Attorneys. Many people who employ attorneys seem to forget the very important fact that these professionals are specialists. Divorce attorneys do divorces. Patent attorneys work with patents. Criminal defense lawyers work with criminal law cases. Real estate attorneys deal with real estate issues.

You want someone who is experienced in the type of business you are launching and the types of issues you are facing. In addition to technical expertise related to your industry, I place a high value on finding someone who is responsive. If they can't return a call or email quickly to help me with whatever my problem is, I am not going to use them.

You also want someone who is competent and detail-oriented so that they don't make mistakes or do things that could get you in trouble with the IRS. I have worked with plenty of bad accountants and attorneys over the years, and it is always costlier than the money saved by using them instead of better-qualified providers.

Accountants. Regardless of your business, you will need good advice on how you set up the legal form for your company based on what you are doing.

If you are into real estate, for instance, do you only flip, or do you hold onto properties that you lease out? The rules for capturing losses and tax treatment of gains are sometimes complex and constantly changing, and you need someone who understands these things. You also may need help with matters such as bonding if you get your contractor's license, as we did at Mark Zweig, Inc. This required meeting certain balance sheet requirements and the proper accounting treatment to show values of properties came into play.

As is the case for most professional service providers, specialization and experience in dealing with businesses like yours are crucial. We have had better success dealing with larger regional firms than small one- or two-person accounting firms because the larger firms have experts in a variety of issues.

Insurance agents. I learned the hard way about the importance of having a good insurance agent.

After years of doing projects, I realized the agent we used was insuring various renovation projects we had underway with rental policies instead of construction policies. If we had a claim due to fire or another disaster when our project was insured with a rental policy, we might not have been covered.

When I confronted the agent with my discovery (thanks to a review of all of our insurance from another agent who is a friend), he said that his firm doesn't offer construction policies. If he was good—and honest—he would have told me that without me asking! Get the right agent who sees you as a long-term client and treats you accordingly.

Title companies. I value long-term relationships with our title company just like I do with our other service providers. They have all of my information, and because they know we are a source of repeat business, they treat our closings as a priority. Also, a good title company gets on things early, so if there are problems, we have time to deal with them before our contracted closing date.

Construction contractors and subcontractors. Finding the right contractors and subcontractors based on project type, location, and ability to perform is one of the most difficult aspects of the development business.

We learned that the larger the project (think commercial or multifamily), the greater the odds we would be able to find and afford to work with competent contractors and subcontractors. On the residential side, however, we struggled for years to find firms or people who were reliable, did quality work, and who didn't overcharge us due to either greed or incompetence.

When you find a firm or person you can work with, it's crucial that they have proper insurance coverage. If they don't, your insurance company will discover it in an audit, and you will be responsible for their insurance costs after the fact.

I like long-term relationships with people I trust. When you have that, you can't price-shop every time you need their services. One thing I know for certain is that these people don't like to bid on every job. Cost estimating takes time away from doing work, and doing work is the only thing they get paid for. Being able to dispatch them quickly and trust that they won't overcharge you is critical if you want to be in this business.

Architects, engineers, and planners. These professionals are also critical to your success in real estate development, especially if your business moves beyond just doing single-family renovation projects. Architects and engineers are specialists, too, and not just anyone is good for any type of project. You will likely need different architects for your commercial projects than you would need for a single-family home.

Some are more versed in historic projects and renovations than new construction. Some have a bent for modern design, and some for more traditional design. Some will work with you and do only what you need, and others will insist on providing a complete package of services.

There are great variations in costs. Engineers don't like small projects. You will need a one-person structural engineer who will help you at times on call, and they aren't always easy to find. You will also need a civil engineering and/or planning firm that is familiar with site-specific planning and permitting issues. Those who just do work for government clients will not be good to use.

It's hard to put a price on good design because it greatly affects construction costs and the ultimate value of the completed project. The right design professionals will be invaluable when it comes to working with the myriad of standards and regulations and zoning issues that you have to address to get a permit. The relationships your design professionals have with the people in the city could determine whether or not you can get your project permitted.

18

Fueling Your Growth

E ntrepreneurship is about value creation, and growth equates to value. Growth creates excitement; it's motivational to the business owners and employees alike. With growth comes new challenges and learning opportunities for everyone. And growth leads to profitability, which means everyone who works for or owns the company can improve their lot.

Most everyone who owns a business will tell you they want their business to grow. For many, unfortunately, that stated desire is what Mike Latas, my boss from forty years ago, called "lip music." These business owners talk a good game, but they fail to actually do what it takes to grow.

What are those things?

It starts with your vision. If you want to grow, you have to set growth goals—*real* growth goals. Not modest goals of 5 percent to 10 percent annually. That's too slow for a new business. Strike out a bold vision. Where do you really want the business to go? How can you do it? How long will it take you to get there? Paint the picture, and put your foot on the accelerator.

Next, you need a disciplined sales process. Consistent results take a consistent process. You can hire all the salespeople you want—experienced or not—but if you don't train and manage those people to do what it takes to meet your sales targets, then they (and you) will fail.

Whatever it is you are selling, the process is essentially the same. There is always a sales funnel, and the more prospects you have at the top of the funnel, the greater the probability of making a sale. Next, define the market—the organizations and people you are trying to sell to—and generate awareness through your direct mail, email, public relations, and social media efforts. Then start contacting potential clients or customers via email and telephone.

The goal is always to advance to the next step in the process—not to make a sale with the first contact (although that *can* happen). Just keep

Going Big

Carter & Burgess, founded in 1939 as a two-man civil engineering and landscape architecture firm, experienced modest growth for several decades, but it really took off when a new CEO set a vision for something many others saw as impossible.

Jerry Allen joined the Fort Worth, Texas–based firm in 1969 when it had forty employees. He was an executive vice president and COO when I joined the company in 1985. The company had been decimated by a real estate recession when Jerry was named president and CEO in 1988, but he remained bullish on its future. In fact, his overarching goal for Carter & Burgess was "2000 by 2000"—two thousand employees by the year 2000.

That seemed like a ridiculous growth goal, but when Jerry died in 2002 following a battle with cancer, Carter & Burgess had 2,300 employees with more than forty offices in twenty-two states, plus operations in Europe. And when the company was sold to publicly held Jacobs Engineering Group in 2010, it had 3,200 employees.

The growth rate made the company valuable. And while it took more than a big goal to make that growth happen, setting his sights on something big gave Jerry and everyone else at Carter & Burgess a mission. They committed to that mission, and they found a way to accomplish it.

advancing your prospect to the next step until that ends up with a buying decision.

Success in selling takes a willingness to meet with people, by phone and in person, and a dogged determination to get results. And if you have a business where the customers come to you, you had best make sure your salespeople know how to treat every one of them and how to close the deal.

In support of your sales efforts, you need to make a higher-than-average investment in marketing and promotion. It's such a simple idea. If the typical firm in your business spends 5 percent on marketing and advertising and you want to grow faster than them, then you should spend two or three times as much. Even in a flat market, this approach applied over time can lead to growth at the expense of your competitors.

You also need to prepare for growth by aggressively and continuously recruiting employees. This involves viewing everyone you meet as a potential employee—someone you want to get to know so that you can see how they might fit in your organization. But it also involves creating a culture where people want to work. If you provide good jobs, people will want to work with you, and you will be able to hire people who can help you grow.

One incentive that helps you find and keep key employees is to share equity with them. There is nothing quite as motivational as owning a piece of the pie. It's the American Dream for so many of us. Real ownership—not options, nonvoting stock, or class Z shares in an LLC only for a specific location—is incredibly valued by your best people. Tie them down or lose them. It's your choice. But it's hard to grow if you are constantly losing your best people.

Those people also need the right tools to grow the business, so invest in your information technology. Good IT makes you more efficient and reduces friction in your customers' or clients' buying experience. That gives you a competitive advantage and helps you grow.

Finally, look for opportunities to acquire competitors so you can spread your overhead over a larger revenue number. An acquisition gets you new customers and a few good employees, too. Smaller firms are typically easier to buy because the seller has fewer options. In fact, the seller may be willing to finance the whole deal. This can be cheaper and faster than only trying to grow internally.

19

Keeping Your Priorities Straight

One of the greatest challenges business owners face is keeping their priorities straight, especially when they are just starting a venture. There are so many things vying for your attention—both inside and outside your business. I have struggled with this most of my life, not just during the start-up stage, and I have not always handled it well.

Entrepreneurs have a tendency to live life with no breaks, often because they feel that they have something to prove (to themselves or to others). They are highly motivated to be successful, and while that's often a good thing, going at full speed all of the time can cause you to make poor decisions, it can be exhausting, it can have a negative effect on your mental and physical health, and it can damage your relationships.

If you have to work long hours in your business, is it fair to spend your nights and weekends doing anything that doesn't involve your family? Most of the time, it isn't. Some people hang out with their friends every evening, spend all weekend golfing, or stay so occupied with their hobbies that there is nothing left for anyone else. Is that how you want to be remembered? Probably not.

Yet, many entrepreneurs can't stop chasing every shiny object that comes across their paths. They can't let go of anything they do. They are better than everyone else at what they do. They make a lot of money doing it. They are admired and respected by their customers, clients, and employees. And they wear their workaholism and obsession with their business (or businesses) like a badge of honor. If you ask them, they will tell you it is "who they are." Work consumes them, and, consequently, they struggle to find inner peace.

Entrepreneurs can be experts at making excuses and justifying their misguided priorities. I know this from personal experience. But I've also learned there are some practical things you can do to straighten out your priorities, get off the merry-go-round, and find some of that elusive inner peace. And the best time to do these practical things is now.

Learn to say *no*. You can't do everything. Saying *no* tactfully is one of the most important skills you can have as an entrepreneur. Saying *yes* gets you to a certain point, but your time isn't limitless.

After too many *yeses*, I learned that you have to say *no* to anything you won't be able to excel at and anything that doesn't enhance your reputation or advance your longer-term goals—bad projects, bad clients, investments that you know will strain your resources and probably won't work.

At times, you also need to say *no* to things you can do and that are worth doing but that you shouldn't do for one reason or another. You can't make donations to every wonderful cause, for instance. Nor can you say yes to every good opportunity that requires an investment of your time or money.

Overcommitment may be a way to make a lot of money, but it is not necessarily the way to be happy. I always said *yes* to every chance to add something to my plate if it could lead to us making more money, and I took pride in my overcommitments. But at some point, having a bigger house and flashier cars and eating at expensive restaurants means nothing. And taking care of all the "stuff" you own creates a ton of stress and distraction. You cannot have inner peace when you are overcommitted. Instead, you will just be stressed and unhappy.

It's not easy to say no for a variety of reasons. But you have to. Listen to your gut. The human computer is far better than most people realize.

Learn to delegate. Many people become entrepreneurs because they want to do something better than others who are providing some product or service. On top of that, their business often starts out undercapitalized, which means cash flow and expenses have to be carefully managed to preserve precious working capital. That makes it hard to let go of anything.

Delegating, however, is good for your mental and physical health. And it's also good for your business and the people who work for you. If you are serious about building a business that has value that you can harvest at some point, then you had better be adept at finding and developing some talented people. I'm talking about people who can do everything you can do and even improve on things without your direction or in your absence.

If you don't delegate, the people you hire won't develop or contribute their full potential. And if they are any good, they eventually will go somewhere else that gives them an opportunity to grow.

Create an identity that is separate from your business. Try to go a year without telling people you meet who you are by connecting it to the work that you do. It's hard. But it's necessary if you want to branch out and have a life outside of your business. If your whole identity is connected with your business and anything bad happens to or in your business, it will be crushing.

Do something tangible with your hands. This forces you out of your normal role as the orchestra conductor and puts you in the role of a doer. That's healthy. Doing something with your hands is always gratifying; plus, it gives you time to reflect and think, which is a value hard to measure.

Limit your mental garbage. Many people become addicted to social media and television news, and that can lead to stress that destroys your inner peace. I am not advocating ignorance. You have to stay informed. But you also have to accept that too much of this stuff—and keep in mind that we all control those channels and what we see and hear—will negatively affect how you view other people, which ultimately will damage your relationship with yourself and with others.

Put your phone down. Today's phones are one of the greatest tools ever created, but they also are a twenty-four-hour source of distraction. Every spare moment we have—and I do mean every moment: stoplights, bathrooms, dull parts of movies, meetings, even conversations with our spouses—are times when a smartphone can fill up with social media, games, YouTube videos, eBay bidding, and shopping.

Get a dog and cat that loves you. Pets are shown to reduce your stress. We have three cats and a one-hundred-forty-pound dog, and they demand my attention. That attention (aside from filling food and water bowls, cleaning litter boxes, and letting the dog in and out) is time spent giving and receiving love. It helps me relax and keep a healthy perspective on what matters in my life.

Exchange your negative, critical attitude for one that's accepting of others. This last point is really, really hard for me. I have been a "boss" for forty years, a management consultant for more than thirty-five years, and a teacher at the university level for more than seventeen years. I have trained myself to be critical and see better ways of doing things.

That's all fine, but it also can cause you to prioritize yourself (your opinions, your wants, your needs) over what's truly best for others and even your business.

If you want inner peace, you must find a way to turn all that off and just be a regular person like everyone else. If you can't, everyone you care about will get sick of you. They will see you as a negative, judgmental know-it-all because they will see that your top priority is yourself.

Where you spend your time and money shows who and what is important to you. When we're younger than sixty, it's been said, we trade our time for money, and when we're older than sixty, we trade our money for time. The problem with that axiom is that money can't always buy you time. Use your time wisely by constantly reminding yourself of what is really important in your life. Think and act according to your real priorities—starting right now!

You Shouldn't Have to Kill Yourself

Ｔhis issue of managing priorities is so important that I want to share a bit more about my personal experience with the struggle in the hopes that you will better understand the mistakes I've made and avoid them as you launch your business.

I see a lot of articles about famous entrepreneurs who talk about how you have to work nonstop to be successful. Maybe you've heard stories about Elon Musk frequently working one-hundred-and-twenty hours a week and sleeping on his factory floor or about how Steve Jobs routinely worked eighty to ninety hours a week.

But is that really necessary to be successful?

I get asked this question frequently by budding entrepreneurs.

My response is that there are many gradients on the success continuum, and not everyone feels the need to be a billionaire. I can imagine it has its pluses, but maybe trading every other aspect of your life for that kind of success isn't worth it to you.

I never set out to be a billionaire, but I worked fifty hours a week in high school, got my undergrad and graduate degrees in four years while working jobs and co-owning a motorcycle shop, and became an owner of an architecture and engineering firm when I was twenty-six. Then I started my primary business in 1988 when I was thirty, married, and had a six-month-old daughter.

I worked really hard.

There were years when I gave as many as fifty talks or seminars, billed close to a couple thousand consulting hours, and was pretty much gone somewhere different every week.

And yes, I was successful by almost any standard. Not Elon Musk successful or Steve Jobs successful, but successful enough that our business grew by an average of 30 percent annually for thirteen straight years, and we got on the *Inc.* 500 list of fastest-growing privately held companies two years in a row.

My wife at the time had her own business, too, a successful reading clinic. And we did well enough financially that we could easily afford a 5,200-square-foot house on six acres abutting the Charles River in one of the most expensive towns in the Boston area. We drove fancy European cars, and I amassed a collection of more than twenty motorcycles. We had lawn people, a full-time nanny, house cleaners, pool maintenance people, snow plowers, and even our own personal house painter on staff. And our kids had trainers for their horses that we boarded at an expensive facility.

But what happened next?

My wife, whom I had been with since I was eighteen, became an alcoholic and prescription drug addict and suffered a mental breakdown. She spent more than ten months in a private rehab facility. We eventually went through a bitter divorce, and I ended up with sole custody of our two young daughters with no contact allowed with their mother. Meanwhile, I had to turn over the reins of my business to my partners because I couldn't do my job.

This all coincided with the 9/11 attacks on our country, and our business completely flattened out. We had it under contract to sell, but our buyers backed out, and we had to slog through three more years in the midst of my personal crisis before finally selling to a private equity firm in 2004.

So while I was financially successful, my complete dedication to my business and abdication of practically all child-rearing and family duties created a lot of problems. We all paid a significant price.

Was it worth the pot of gold we got at the end of the rainbow that allowed me to essentially retire at age forty-six? Will these kinds of problems develop for everyone who works like that to build their businesses? You tell me.

Since then, I have been fortunate enough to become a teacher at the Sam M. Walton College of Business at the University of Arkansas. I bought back my business (in a decimated state), turned it around with the help of a good friend (who later would become my third wife), started another business that became successful and got on the *Inc.* 5000 list, and had two more daughters. Then my second wife and I divorced, and I later resold my ownership interest in my original business.

In short, I repeated some, if not all, of the mistakes I made the first time around.

I am now fortunate enough to have my third wife—someone who absorbed the entire responsibility for my other business (a one-time *Inc.*

5000 development and construction company). She, too, worked a ton of hours to get that business under control while I worked in my original business and at the UA. It nearly killed her in the process, and she also paid a price in her personal life. It was too much.

Today, I devote my time to teaching and working with a few long-time clients, and we are winding down our development and construction business.

But we have time. Time to think. Time to reflect. Time to pick up my second crop of kids from school. Time to take walks. Time to read books. Time to spend on small home improvement projects. Time to spend one-on-one with my students and former students. Time to spend with our dog.

I prefer to define *success* as how much control I have over my time each day and with whom I spend my time. While I make a lot less money than I was making twenty-five years ago, I am much happier. It's not a rationalization, either. All of that sacrifice to keep living in larger and larger houses and buy more toys was not worth the price I paid.

My mission now is to spend the rest of my life sharing what I have learned along this journey to help other people. To the extent I can do that, while at the same time having a life I truly enjoy on a daily basis, avoiding the temptation of pursuing unending material acquisition and ego glorification will be my definition of *success*.

Don't get me wrong. Building a business doesn't necessarily have to destroy your personal life or lead to an early death. You can balance all of it if you are thoughtful about the type of business you build and how you spend your time. Sure, you may have to work until nine o'clock some nights. But then maybe you can get home by two on another day. You need that time for other things. You also need time to think and reflect. It's essential to achieving work/life balance—or better yet—work/life integration.

It is possible.

You may not be the next Elon Musk or Steve Jobs, and that's OK. You could actually be more successful than them—successful in life. Just remember that no one on their deathbed ever said they wished they had worked more hours!

PART III

The E-Life

Comedian Steven Wright, who is known for his dry wit and stoic delivery, sets up one of his jokes by telling the audience he is writing a book.

"I've got the page numbers done," he says, "so now I just have to fill in the rest."

Starting a business can feel similar. Getting the structure right is important, but at that point, the hard work has just begun. You still have to fill in those blank pages each and every day when it comes to things like leadership, marketing, sales, customer service, strategy, employee relationships, building teams, dealing with economic crises, and developing a leadership pipeline.

So this part of the book provides some insights and advice on the things entrepreneurs must routinely do to keep their businesses going and growing. In other words, it's all about how to write the book that will become your business.

When You Have an Old Car—Or Business

I have always been a car guy. Old cars, new cars—even cars that we built from the ground up with an entirely new chassis, steel body, and 320 cubic inch Buick Straight-8 engine.

I have owned somewhere north of four hundred cars in my lifetime, and I've found that cars are kind of like businesses: They need constant attention.

My current daily driver is a 1999 Rolls-Royce Silver Spur—one of the last seventy "real" Rolls-Royces—that was hand-built at Crewe, England. To say it always needs something is a vast understatement. While not that expensive to buy—at least compared with what it would cost new— it's *very* expensive to keep going. And there are always little chores to attend to if I don't want problems to get out of hand.

The same holds true for a business, so we need to cover some of the routine maintenance issues that will help keep your business from becoming another jalopy that's broken down on the side of the road. This is a high-level checklist; I'll go into some of these in more detail in subsequent chapters.

Promote your purpose. Recent studies have shown that purpose is more important than passion when it comes to keeping people engaged with their work. It is especially important to younger people who want meaning in their work. I also think it is important to older people who have achieved some degree of material success but have realized that they want more from life.

Having a worthwhile mission is crucial to your long-term success, but only if that purpose is shared throughout the organization so that everyone can feed off its energy. Don't assume everyone knows that purpose or that they are connecting all the dots between what they do, what the company does, and why it all matters.

Make planning part of the culture. Business plans aren't just for start-ups. Get everyone involved in the planning process, and make sure every decision is consistent with the mission, vision, goals, and strategies. Consistently sharing progress toward goals helps everyone feel like they are on the same team and gives a warning when things are starting to go off track.

Make innovation and improvement a management obsession. Achieving excellence means there has to be a relentless pursuit of improvement. If the organization is going to remain competitive in the markets it serves, it must keep improving every single aspect of everything it does. That means "breaking what may not be broken" and "good enough isn't good enough" should be regularly repeated mantras throughout your business.

Check in with key clients and customers. I can't tell you how many small business owners I have observed over the years who lost touch with their clients and customers. They didn't keep up with their customers' and clients' needs or with how well their business was meeting those needs. Then they lose interest in their business as a result.

Pick up the phone and make some calls. Get on the customer service desk. Talk to customers on the floor if you have a retail business. Reacquaint yourself with your customers and their wants and needs.

Talk to your employees. The longer a business operates and the larger it gets, the more likely leaders are to take their people for granted. These owners lose touch with the problems and frustrations their people are encountering as they go about their daily work. But when you regularly engage in conversations with your people on their turf (versus telling them to come to you), you show them a respect that opens them to communication and makes them more receptive to your leadership.

Talk to your bank. Banking relationships need periodic attention, too. Keeping them informed of what is going well and what isn't going so well is critical if you want them to be there when you need them.

Even though banking is a highly regulated industry, I've found that community banks are much more tuned in to your needs and better able to assist you because you can have real relationships with their top people. These relationships, like all relationships, take maintenance. That means you have to spend some time on them and make sure all lines of communication remain open. Banking is more critical than ever because debt capital is affordable and should almost always be your first source to go to for funding.

Talk to your accountants. Staying in touch with your outside accountants helps you make better decisions for yourself and your business. For example, we once took out a loan in the name of our company, but it was secured by personal assets. The net effect of that decision cost us more than a hundred thousand dollars in taxes that we wouldn't have had to pay had we chosen a different path. Any competent CPA would have seen the error of our ignorance, so we paid the price for not regularly communicating with our outside accountants.

Know your numbers. Whether you are talking to bankers and accountants or employees on the front lines of your business, you need to know exactly where the company stands financially. That means you need to have good accounting and financial management practices so that you know your cash flow situation and so you have accurate forecasting.

Knowing exactly what your costs are and who and what is making money (and what isn't making money) is key to making decisions that drive revenues and profits. But don't fall into the habit of just looking at the big picture. Some products, for instance, might not be profitable on their own but might be worth keeping because they lead to sales of other more profitable offerings. Sometimes it is necessary to sell certain things or provide certain services so that customers or clients don't go elsewhere for everything else they need. This is always a challenge, and it's a challenge you likely won't meet if you aren't familiar with your financials.

Look at your facilities. When business owners develop blindness toward their facilities and workplaces, they allow things to run down, and they tolerate situations that make people uncomfortable. It's important to continuously evaluate the uses and functionality of your spaces, whether they are offices, industrial, or retail, so that you will know where maintenance or upgrades are needed.

Review what you pay people. I have never been a fan of regularly scheduled pay reviews for employees—at least the way most organizations do it, which is once or twice a year. A better approach is to make pay changes continuously as needed.

The whole notion that someone gets hired into a job in a company and then gets 0–7 percent annual raises is archaic. That's like setting sail and never course-correcting due to different winds. What individuals get paid—if you truly want to be fair with them and recognize their contributions and worth to the organization—takes continuous monitoring and maintenance.

Reward cooperation and flexibility. As the organization changes and evolves, so must the roles and responsibilities of the people who work there. That's why employees who are too rigid and expect concrete job descriptions aren't the best types to have on the team. But you can use accounting and incentive compensation schemes to reward cooperation rather than creating unhealthy internal competition. Cooperation needs to be recognized and rewarded and be part of the firm's culture.

Remember (and share) what got you here. As time passes, there's a tendency to forget, and then stop doing, many of the things that were critical to your success. And second-generation managers often want to make their mark by dropping or modifying strategies that were instrumental in the firm's early success. At times, of course, those strategies need to be dropped or revised. But founders have to properly coach, mentor, and guide their successors to avoid critical strategic blunders that can hurt the business.

Like my old Rolls-Royce (and dozens of other cars I have owned), your business is more likely to run at its best if you constantly and continuously care for it. And that is your job as the owner.

When Good People Don't Get Along

I f you ask anyone who has owned a business for any length of time what keeps them up at night, chances are they will tell you it involves "people problems." It's not making payroll, sweating over a big sale, or any of the other stuff that is strategically or tactically critical to your firm's success. Nope, it's friction among people.

One of the most frustrating problems for business owners is when two productive employees don't get along. One decides that they are making all the money for the business. Or one decides that the other person isn't working as hard as they are. Or one of them thinks the other disrespected them in a meeting. Or someone thinks that the other person is being treated better than they are.

The causes are numerous, but the result is the same: Conflict.

You might be tempted to take the two people who aren't getting along and bang their heads together the way Moe would do with Larry and Curly on an episode of *The Three Stooges*, but that is not possible—or effective.

So what can you do?

First, some preventative maintenance may be in order. Are you hiring the right people in the first place? Did you check their references? And if you do see signs that someone is too competitive or too negative about other people, do you pull them aside and address it immediately? Maybe you can keep some of these relationship problems from getting out of hand if you act early.

Second, are you sure you aren't showing favorites or creating the impression that you have favorites? I have created problems for myself by doing this. I was really high on someone who was doing a great job, and I told everyone around me how great they were. But instead of reinforcing the right kinds of behaviors, it made other people jealous. They started to dislike the one who, in my eyes, was a "star." It's important to recognize people for their good work, but be careful not to overpromote someone.

In the same way, be careful not to talk about other people in a negative way. You could inadvertently create a culture where people are too critical and judgmental. This can be toxic, and I have to fight my natural tendencies in this area.

Third, do all that you can to build strong teams. Do you need to go on a ropes course together? Would an escape room experience be in order? Go on a canoe trip together? Some other team-building exercise? These things may seem hokey, but they often help people form more productive relationships. (More on this in chapter 23.)

Fourth, if a "not getting along" situation does develop, investigate it and hear everyone out. Sometimes people are upset for a good reason. A mistake a lot of managers make is assuming that a complaint isn't legitimate because of preconceived notions about specific people or situations. If someone did do something that hurt the other person's feelings, maybe you should bring that up to the offender and suggest they try to make amends.

Fifth, be careful about the things you measure, report on, and reward. The scorecard you keep could be a major factor in creating problems. You can't quantitatively measure some contributions, especially over the short term. People don't always see the long-term results of other people's efforts. And overhead allocations to determine the profitability of one area of the business over another can be arbitrary. There are many complex interrelationships that need to be acknowledged.

Make sure your raise and bonus programs don't reinforce the wrong things. If they are too slanted toward individual performance and group/team/department/office performance versus company-wide performance, you could end up with too much internal competition. My preferred practice is to pay out most of the bonus money based on how the company performed overall versus how individuals did their jobs.

Finally, promote the idea of "one for all and all for one." Bring up the issue at meetings. Talk about it, including the idea that various units do well at different times. Talk about how having one product or service line that is ostensibly not as profitable as another still benefits everyone. Talk about success stories of cooperation between people or across organizational lines and how that accomplished something they couldn't have gotten done otherwise. Maybe you should even go as far as putting "One company for all" on all internal communications.

This is important stuff. We all need our sleep. So do what you can to head off or mitigate problems that are keeping you awake!

23

Reaping What You Sow with Employee Engagement

E mployee engagement has been a trendy topic in business for several years, and for good reason. Employees who are committed and connected to your company's purpose are more productive, more loyal, less likely to bolt for another job, and their engagement drives customer satisfaction and improves your firm's reputation.

When employees aren't engaged—and research continually shows that most employees aren't—then it's up to you, as the founder and leader of your company, to do something about it. And complaining doesn't count as "doing something."

All too often, I hear leaders bashing their employees, especially younger employees, for their lack of engagement and commitment. This approach improves the situation by exactly 0 percent. In fact, it usually makes it worse.

Sure, employees have a responsibility to come to work with a positive attitude and to do their best in their jobs, but leaders must lead the way. And if your employees aren't as engaged as you'd like them to be, the first place to look for solutions is in the mirror. You are probably treating most, if not all, of your employees in ways that are creating the results you are seeing. You shouldn't expect anything different from them unless you treat them differently.

Here are some of the biggest reasons I've found that employees aren't as engaged, motivated, and committed as their leaders would like. Note that some of these involve the type of maintenance outlined in previous chapters. That's because employee engagement isn't a one-time event; it's an ongoing process that takes time, energy, and intentionality.

You don't talk to them enough. Some business owners still operate with the antiquated notion that you can't be friends with your employees.

Therefore, they don't talk with them enough out of fear the employees will start thinking they are friends and taking advantage of them. This is bad thinking.

Employees will always care more and perform better when they think their boss actually cares about them. Showing that care will help your employees care about you. It's a normal human reaction.

No doubt, some managers let their personal feelings about specific employees cloud their judgment. I am sure I have done that a time or two, but the benefits of befriending your people outweigh the cost. If you aren't friends with your employees and don't really know them as individuals, they will be less inclined to trust you. And high trust levels between management and employees will supercharge your business's performance.

You have an "us-against-them" culture. The feeling that all employees other than management are a necessary evil and everyone is replaceable inevitably leads to an unhealthy culture. When the employees feel oppressed and expendable, you aren't going to get their best, just as you wouldn't give your best if treated that way.

You don't involve them in your business planning. Maybe your people aren't engaged because you haven't included them in the enterprise. That requires that you listen to their thoughts and input when it comes to the mission, strategies, goals, and action items that are part of your planning process. Being part of the planning effort will help them feel more connected to the business and what you are trying to accomplish.

You don't have a meaningful mission or vision. If you want an engaged workforce, you have to have a reason for existing and a primary goal beyond just making a profit that enriches your bank account. If your employees think that money is your main mission, it will be hard to keep them motivated, engaged, and enthusiastic about the company and their jobs.

People want to work for a business that stands for something and is doing some kind of good for society or a segment of it. Your job is to articulate just what that is and make it a reality. The extent to which you can create a purpose-driven organization will determine how engaged your employees really are.

You don't share financial information. It's crazy, but many small business owners do not tell their employees how the business is doing and don't provide them with any specific numbers showing the financial performance of the enterprise.

Studies show that when you don't give your employees any financial information, they assume you are making much, much more money than you actually are from the business. If employees think you are rolling in dough, is it any wonder they are upset and unmotivated? And if they don't see what is working and what isn't, how can you expect them to be working to solve your problems? It's completely unrealistic to think that.

You don't commit to sharing a portion of the profits. Along with not sharing the numbers, many small business owners don't share profits with their workers, either. When that's the case, there are absolutely no incentives that encourage people to do anything beyond the least they have to do to keep their jobs.

There are no consequences for those who aren't engaged. I think this is the case because so many business owners know deep down that they aren't the best employers. They don't show any real care for their people, but they also don't want to have to replace anyone unless the employee's behavior is so egregious that they have absolutely no choice. No rewards and no sanctions. Not the way to motivate and engage your employees with the company!

You aren't as engaged as you should be. Maybe you have lost interest in your business and have stopped caring as much as you should. How will any employee be engaged with their work and company if the owners of the enterprise aren't engaged and committed themselves? They won't be. It's unrealistic. Owners have to set an example.

There's an old saying that if we reap what we sow, most of us should pray for crop failure. You are reaping what you are sowing in terms of employee motivation, engagement, and commitment. Try sowing better seeds, and better results will follow.

24

Building Teams

When I began teaching classes on entrepreneurship and new venture development, I let my students form their own new business planning teams at the beginning of the semester. After a few years, however, I decided I would assign them to teams.

Why?

I do it to ensure there is some diversity on the teams.

When they self-selected, we would have five frat brother marketing majors, and their ideas weren't very creative. In fact, the least creative teams I had were the most homogeneous and culturally compatible.

For example, one planning team came up with an idea to create a koozie for Mickey's Big Mouth Malt Liquor because, at the time, it had an odd bottle shape. And because they were all duck hunters, they wanted to use a camouflage pattern and a design based on the shape of the state of Texas. They couldn't understand that they would have a very small market potential with that idea because to each of them, it sounded like something they'd buy. No diversity and cultural compatibility led to myopia. I have witnessed the same thing in firms where the owners and key people all had similar backgrounds and ways of thinking.

Diversity doesn't just mean different sexes or ethnic backgrounds, even though those are important. It also can mean different academic or experience backgrounds or different discipline expertise.

For example, early in my career, I worked for an engineering firm as the head of project development (another term for *marketing*) and human resources. I was the first nontechnical person who was part of the executive team and the first nonengineer to become an owner. I saw lots of room for improvement in the ways we did things at that company, so I pushed for changes. When I eventually turned in my notice to join a larger, more successful firm, my boss, the chairman and CEO, said if anyone ever asked him about me, he would tell them I was "a s***-disturber, but that they needed their s*** disturbed."

I don't think I realized what a compliment that was at the time! But really, it may have been as simple as the fact that I was not culturally compatible with the rest of the owners.

Cultural compatibility may stifle disagreement, but disagreement is sometimes necessary. You need people who will challenge you and your assumptions about things. It doesn't mean you will always love those people, nor does it necessarily mean they will always stay with you over the long haul.

I won't deny that I don't usually love having my ideas or ways that I do things challenged—at least at first. It can be very uncomfortable. But I do think it is often necessary if you want your business to move ahead and take on a life of its own and develop real leaders who can keep things going in a positive direction after you are gone.

There are two main talent pools when building effective teams. One is to assemble them from the workers you already have, and the other is to bring in new people with skills and experiences your existing team lacks.

As the owner of a business, you should constantly be on the lookout for talent, and not just the people with very specific types of education, certification, or licensure. Sometimes you just need an intelligent person who is honest and has good communication skills and work ethic. When you are looking for good people, it's amazing how often you will find them. And when you find them, you can recruit them to join your team.

Many times, however, you can build your team with the talent already in the organization, which is why it's so important to really know what different people do well and what they don't do so well.

You also have to consider fit—how new members of a team will get along with existing team members, whether they have complementary technical skills, and how their personalities will mesh. You don't want a team full of visionaries and no doers, for instance, or a team full of people who love to get things done but have no vision for the future. Another important aspect of creating successful teams is picking the right people to lead them, regardless of whether it's a standing business unit or a group that's pulled together for a short-term project.

Selecting who will be formally assigned a leadership role is never easy. But it may be easier than you think if you approach it differently. Instead of

Leading a Team of Experts

A person who is good at doing something is not necessarily going to be a good leader. The best salesperson may not be the best sales manager, or the best engineer may not be the best leader of a team. On the other hand, leading people who do something that you aren't good at doing yourself is never easy. People want to work for leaders who have been in their shoes and have some deeper understanding of the work.

So what happens when you need to lead a team and you don't share their expertise?

J. K. Symancyk, who became CEO of PetSmart in 2018, says the answer is found in developing the ability to "exercise authority without having to be an expert in everything."[1]

When Symancyk was a guest on a podcast hosted by Walton College Dean Matt Waller, he shared a story about leading a team that was opening fresh meat and produce departments for Sam's Club stores in Mexico. He was chosen for the role because he had some international experience and he spoke Spanish, but he had no experience with fresh foods.

"I was learning on a Tuesday what I might be trying to teach somebody on a Wednesday," he said. "Not at all qualified, but it was such a fast education."[2]

Symancyk realized he had to teach the Walmart/Sam's Club business models while also being vulnerable enough to learn from others.

"It was probably one of the best training grounds for being in a position (now) where, ultimately, I end up having to make a lot of decisions where I have to lean on the expertise of people who are much deeper in the subject than I am," he told Waller, "and know how to exercise judgment when I may not have the time to go as deep as I would love to go on some of the subjects that I have to weigh in on."[3]

1. J. K. Symancyk and Matt Waller, "J. K. Symancyk Shares the Importance of Continual Learning and Saying 'Yes' to New Experiences," February 24, 2021, BeEPIC Podcast, Episode 112, https://walton.uark.edu/be-epic-podcast/jk -symancyk.php.
2. Symancyk and Waller, "Continual Learning."
3. Symancyk and Waller, "Continual Learning."

basing your decisions on seniority, the existing organizational hierarchy, or who is next in line, do so instead on who is already demonstrating an ability to lead other people.

I was reminded of this recently when a client in the professional services business skipped over all of their existing partners and elevated a younger and more dynamic person to the president's job. The person they picked is more energetic, committed, and a better communicator than anyone in the partner ranks and is already taking the company in new positive directions.

Loosening the Reins

Many entrepreneurs start new ventures because they are unhappy with the offerings of current providers and think they can do better. This belief—in themselves and in what they think the market needs—fuels a passion that often turns into an obsession that results in early success.

Clients and customers can always recognize when a business is led by someone who really cares, even if they cannot put their finger on exactly why it seems better. It just is. The facilities are cleaner. Problems and complaints are heard and quickly acted on. The employees look better and seem happier. The product is more attractively packaged. Questions get an immediate response. The graphic image and branding are more attractive and authentic. The website is well laid out and easier to navigate. The business has a positive energy. To both outsiders and insiders, the business seems to be running smoothly on all eight cylinders.

All the hard work and attention to detail it takes to create such success, however, inevitably grows beyond the founder's ability to maintain on his or her own. The obsession with attention to detail and personal involvement in everything must give way to delegation. The control freak must loosen the reins.

This shift is not easy, but it is necessary for the long-term health and success of your venture.

So how can you give up control of the things that made you successful?

There's only one answer: You have to impart these same values and sense of caring to every single employee and then back off so that they will learn that you won't step in if they don't do something that needs to be done.

This isn't something that happens overnight, so here are some ideas on how to develop a culture that allows others to flourish and you, as the leader, to comfortably and confidently give up some of your control.

Explain the why. Spend a great deal of time talking to people so that they understand why certain things are important. The higher they are in your organizational structure, the more time you need to spend explaining your thinking and how you got where you are. When you consistently explain the reasons behind your decisions, you gain confidence that the people around you understand what you want and why and that you will trust them to act accordingly when you aren't around.

For example, you may want to buy a small company in another city that serves a client base that's different from the one your firm currently serves. Your top managers may not understand why you would want to do that. Everything inside the company isn't working perfectly, and they can't understand why you would want to add potential problems.

At this point, you, as the leader, may have to explain your reasoning, which could include points such as that it diversifies the company and reduces your risk, it creates new job opportunities for your people to go to another location, and it makes the company more valuable because it accelerates your growth rate.

Share the victories and problems. Whether it is through company-wide meetings, conference calls, or firm-wide emails, recognize and build up the people who are doing the right things in the right ways. Not only should you make them the heroes of the day, but also share the stories of where things went wrong (without specifically naming the people involved) and get employee input on what should have happened and how to avoid those things in the future.

Promote and reward the people who are doing what you want. One simple definition of corporate culture is that it's all about the behaviors that are rewarded or punished. You have to be sure the real performers are the ones who are getting ahead. And these are not necessarily the people you like best!

Share performance metrics. Cash and accrual profits and losses, web hits, client inquiry data, sales information, client satisfaction scores—this information and potentially much more should be shared with all employees so that there is no doubt whether you are doing well or poorly. Everyone needs to feel good or feel the pain, whichever is appropriate based on the metrics.

Share the rewards of your success. I am a huge fan of paying out profits to all employees on either a monthly or quarterly basis (see chapter 12).

Doing What Only You Can Do

Elise Mitchell started a public relations firm in Fayetteville, Arkansas, grew it into a national powerhouse, and eventually sold it to a global brand. She went from being the only employee to a CEO with dozens of full-time staff and a network of contractors. And she eventually discovered that she had to loosen the reins and focus on the things that only she could do.

"The larger an organization grows, the more it needs and depends on specialists rather than generalists," she wrote in her book, *Leading Through the Turn*. "As a leader, you may know how to do lots of things, but that doesn't mean you need to regularly do them all. So what things should you do? The things only you can do and that bring the greatest value to the business."[1]

When she first made this shift, she thought she had delegated herself out of a job. Then she wrote a list of the things only she, as CEO, could do, and that list quickly grew to fourteen priorities. She realized, for instance, that she had been too busy managing growth to focus on a growth plan and that she lacked the understanding she needed about finances.

The shift helped her as a leader, but it also helped the leaders around her and the organization. Other leaders brought different perspectives and abilities to the challenges, they grew personally and professionally, and they were more satisfied with their work.

"On the other hand," she warned, "if you don't truly release leaders— if you don't empower, equip, and enable them—you'll discover that the talented, capable, smart people you worked so hard to get on your team will soon leave for some other team. And they should, because you aren't providing opportunities for them to reach their destinations and enjoy their journeys. Why would anyone stay with somebody who's selfish, driven by power, and hungry for credit?"[2]

Why indeed. Loosen the reins and let your team run free.

---

1. Elise Mitchell, *Leading Through the Turn*, New York, McGraw-Hill Education, 2017, p. 240.
2. Mitchell, *Leading Through the Turn*, p. 103.

Annually is not frequent enough for many reasons. If someone is there and contributing, they should benefit from the firm's success. If they are there and not contributing, they need to either be quickly reformed or let go.

Hire the right people and put them in the right positions. This is one of your top responsibilities—getting more good people to throw in with you and join your team. You cannot delegate this function until you are a significant enterprise. Even then, you shouldn't give it up entirely. It's just too important.

Cut the cancer. The more you depend on others to share or take over the work of leading your company, the more important it is to rid the organization of people who don't embrace your values and culture. Why let them be a cancer on the team? These people aren't the ones you'll ever want to trust with more leadership responsibilities, and their negative energy and comments will undermine the work of those you do trust and count on. It's best for them and you to clear the seat for someone else who does buy into what you are trying to do.

Shift your focus to "what's next?" If you aren't looking ahead at what it will take to keep the business competitive and growing, who will? Too many founders get caught up in the day-to-day operations and don't pay enough attention to coming up with new products, services, and processes—all based on an intimate knowledge of what the company's clients and customers want and need and how everything works inside the business.

Let's face it. What got you there yesterday may not be what it takes to be successful today. You have to find a way to multiply yourself if you want to keep growing. You have to keep growing if you want to provide continuing opportunities for your people. And you must also develop a strong second tier if you ever want to get out and harvest the rewards for all this hard work—one of the core tenants of entrepreneurship.

26

Obsessing over the Quality of Your Customer Service

Imagine you own a fast-food restaurant, and poor customer service costs you a $10 sale. No big deal, right? You don't want to lose a sale, but it's only $10. But what if that customer was spending an average of $10 a week with you as a regular, satisfied patron and, because of that one bad experience, decides never to return. Now your lost revenues start to add up.

It gets worse, of course, when you factor in the consequences of the customer's negative reviews—online and in-person with friends and family.

You cannot put a value on the benefits of great customer service. Creating a buzz in the marketplace of clients or customers who have been treated extraordinarily well does wonders for your brand's reputation. Conversely, stories of unresolved problems or brusque treatment by employees can do lasting damage.

Great customer service takes process, training, communication, and an understanding of the lifetime value of the customer by everyone in the firm because few businesses can survive without returning customers.

Every business owner better be concerned with the quality of what their firm does and how they service their clients and customers.

Let me rephrase that.

Every business owner better be *obsessed* with the quality of what their firm does and how they treat their clients and customers.

What does such an obsession look like?

It can take many forms, of course.

At Mark Zweig, Inc., for instance, we did construction projects. Most were for ourselves as speculators and developers, but a small percentage of our work was done for clients. Either way, I went to every jobsite as frequently as possible, or our quality immediately suffered.

The potential problems were nearly endless—jobsites got messy, a carpenter would trim out a closet incorrectly, there was a tool we needed to fix or replace, the painters would paint something the wrong color, the electricians would wire the light switches in an inconvenient way. Worse yet was when a client who was paying us for labor on a cost-plus basis shared a story about coming to the jobsite and seeing someone take a two-hour lunch or staying on their phone all day.

Even if you aren't in the construction business, you need to get out on the floor and look at what your people are doing. Does it meet your standard? What are your people telling you about how clients and customers are reacting to what your business does for them? The lower in the organization you go, the more you will learn.

Another way to do quality control on your customer service is to do every job in your company. Rolf Wilkin, owner of the Eureka Pizza chain of restaurants, is a great example of a long-term business owner who gets into every aspect of his business. Rolf paints the bathrooms, makes pizzas, and delivers pizzas. One day, I was on the University of Arkansas campus and saw him hawking pizzas to students who were in line at one of the cafeterias!

Most people who have owned businesses for nearly thirty years—significant businesses in terms of their employment and revenue—are far too isolated from the work of the enterprise. Rolf has often told me (and others) you can "learn more from painting the bathroom than doing anything else."

Getting into every role is a great chance to identify quality and service problems that you just can't find through other means. And it will also put you squarely on the front line with clients and customers so you can see firsthand their satisfaction (or lack of it) with your product or service.

An obvious way to see how you are doing with customers and clients is to actually review what shows up in your customer service inbox. I sold a business to a private equity firm that subsequently lost it to their lenders. When the lender recruited me to help turn around the business (we later bought it back from them), one of the first things I did was to gain access to what we called the "customer service inbox." What an eye-opener it was to see the high number of complaints about people not getting products they had purchased, complaining about quality or service issues, or asking questions that weren't being addressed. Knowing those complaints helped us identify the things that badly needed fixing.

Some customers, of course, complain by returning what they bought and getting a refund, so it's also a good idea to see what's coming back to your company. I once bought a 3D printer for my kids from a company called Toybox, and it was defective. They sent us a replacement, but it, too, didn't work. When I contacted them about my repeat problems, they told me several people were having similar problems and that they were being fixed. They asked if we wanted our money back or wanted to give them one more chance. I opted for the latter. The third printer they sent has not had a single issue. Knowing these kinds of problems are going on is essential, but too many owners don't have a clue until it's too late.

Many businesses use surveys to gauge the quality of their customer service, but for me, that's table stakes. The best way to know what clients and customers are thinking about your business is to talk to them face-to-face. If you can't visit with them in person, talk to them on the phone. But don't hide from them. Ask them what they like and don't like about whatever they are buying from you. Ask them what you can do better. Ask open-ended questions and listen to their responses.

In my experience, the preponderance of business owners are afraid to ask their customers or clients how they feel about their product or service because they could get bad news. Burying your head in the sand is never a path to success.

Secret shoppers can also give you a valuable glimpse into how well your business is performing. My friend Mike Stennett owns a dozen franchise restaurants in Arkansas, and he pays secret shoppers to pose as patrons and report to him about their experiences as it develops. When a problem emerges, he addresses it with his managers instantly.

Owners can't be secret shoppers (unless they are shopping online), but they can be a client or customer of their business. Use or consume your own products or services. More CEOs should do that before they become ex-CEOs. If they did, they would spot quality and service problems that could be quickly fixed. More than once, I have experienced what our clients experience in building or renovating my personal houses. I can honestly say that every time I used our company's services and people, I learned something about how we could do things better.

My final suggestion is to look in the trash and see what waste is being generated. Waste is not only costly, but it is indicative of quality problems, so take a look at what is being thrown out and why.

27

A Strategy for Strategic Planning

E ntrepreneurs typically understand the need for a well-crafted strategy for launching and growing their new business, but strategic planning all too often becomes less of a priority once a business becomes established. Every business of every size, however, needs well-crafted, well-communicated strategies that guide its daily operations and decision-making.

A strategy isn't your mission or your action items; it's your philosophy of business. And if you don't know your philosophy of business, you aren't likely to succeed for very long. Thus, strategic planning is not a one-time event but an ongoing circular process that includes three key phases: creating, communicating, and reviewing.

Creating Your Strategies

Your business needs strategies for everything it does—marketing, recruiting, leadership transition, information sharing, quality, customer service, and every other area that's critical to your success. All of these strategies should align with and support the overarching strategy of your business.

Developing good strategies often takes some outside help because it's not something managers usually do on a daily basis. Specialized strategic planning consultants can provide the necessary processes and specific guidance. I recommend finding consultants who not only have significant strategic planning experience but also have experience working for firms in your industry. Less learning at your expense.

Regardless of who drives the planning process, make sure you get input from all of your employees, clients, customers, and suppliers on what they think the organization does well and what they think the organization can improve on. Then break the planning process into two main parts—the strategic plan and the annual operational business plan.

The strategic plan includes your mission (why you are in business), your vision (what you are trying to become by some point in the future), and your strategies (your philosophy or approach to something the organization does).

The annual operational business plan includes quantifiable and measurable goals and very specific action items (specific tasks assigned to someone with dates to accomplish them by).

Communicating Your Strategies

Managers can have a natural bias toward action, and some see the strategic planning process as a navel-gazing exercise, so it's no wonder that decisions often get made that contradict what a firm's top management really wants to do. Problems also pop up when top managers have unresolved differences about what the strategies should be.

Either way, when managers and their employees aren't executing against shared strategies, it can result in wasted money, embarrassment, or needless conflict among employees, and the company is unlikely to achieve its short- or long-range goals.

The root of the problem typically can be found in poor communication.

As strange as it might seem, many leaders invest a great deal of time creating their strategies only to treat them like something that should be locked in a high-security vault. They have clearly defined strategies that are never clearly shared with frontline managers or employees.

In other cases, the strategy is shared, but it's meaningless to the employees because it includes too many clichés and it's so watered down that the philosophy could apply to any business. A lack of clarity results in the strategies being ignored.

Whatever strategies are adopted, communicate them to every employee along with some background on why they were developed and why they are crucial to your success. Also communicate how they will be implemented or practiced on a daily basis. This will make them much more meaningful and increase your odds of success in making them real.

Communicating about strategy needs a strategy of its own. In other words, think through all the different ways, formal and informal, to effectively share this vital information. One memo on the topic won't cut it. The strategy should be introduced in formal ways, with ongoing opportunities for adding detail and answering questions. You can talk about it in emails, town hall meetings, and team meetings, and you might want a specific page on your website that makes it easy for employees to review.

Reviewing Your Strategies

Your mission, vision, and strategies should remain relatively consistent over time, but you should review your strategies at least once a year to evaluate whether they need modifications or need to be thrown out entirely.

There are times when a radical change in strategy could be in order. At some point, you might achieve the vision and adopt something more ambitious, in which case you'll need to change your strategies. Or maybe there's a disruption in the market caused by consumer trends, new technologies, or actions by your competitors.

There are plenty of examples of major strategy changes that were pivotal to a company's success. Apple shifted from being a computer maker to becoming an electronic device maker, for instance, and Netflix went from a strategy of mailing DVDs to a digital electronic platform. And there are examples of companies that stubbornly stuck with certain strategies for too long and didn't survive.

At the same time, because strategies are overarching and impact everything, you need to be careful not to radically change them too often.

Early in my career, I became a junior partner in an engineering firm in Memphis that focused on business in the Mid-South region. Then management impulsively decided to become a full-service architecture and engineering firm. They acquired a Nashville-based architectural firm and adopted a growth strategy of using any project that took us out of the Mid-South as a jumping-off point to create a new office.

We quickly added offices in Anchorage, Alaska, and Seattle, Washington, with plans to add even more. After about six months, however, problems developed in our relationship with the Nashville firm. We divested them and once again decided to be a Mid-South-focused firm. By then, we had a lot of investment in the new national plan, with people and overhead commitments that made it hard to undo quickly. The firm struggled for several years to make a profit, and the employees (myself included) were confused by our schizophrenic changes in strategy.

An Abbreviated Example

To get a better feel for strategic planning, consider this abbreviated example for a start-up T-shirt company.

Mission: We exist to make the best quality, most comfortable, and longest-lasting T-shirts in the world.

Vision: By 2030, we will be a company with $5 million in annual sales and will be recognized as one of the best places to work in the state of Arkansas.

Strategies:

- Sell all of our unique products online through our own website directly to the consumer.
- Use social media and influencer marketing to generate awareness of our company and our products.
- Build a strong brand through having large signage on our building, employees wearing our products, wrapped vehicles, and relentless PR.
- Share the fruits of our labor through a companywide profit distribution based on cash-basis profits that are paid monthly to all employees.
- Maintain a strong financial position through retention of 25–40 percent of our profits annually.

Goals:

- Achieve $1.5 million in sales during 2022.
- Get, at minimum, three articles published in the general print media about our business and what we are doing over the course of 2022.

Actions:

- Hire someone knowledgeable about social media marketing and SEO. Shannon Brubaker to handle NLT 4.1.2022.
- Fully implement the Zoho customer and potential customer database and have it available to all employees through their computers or phones. Jill Savage to handle NLT 7.1.2022.

Personally, I have always admired businesses with a strategy that survives years or even decades with very few significant changes. These companies don't necessarily have large markets, but they have niches that allow them to do well in crowded, mature markets and charge a premium price for what they sell.

There are several shoe companies in Northampton, England, for instance, that still make shoes exactly as they were made two hundred years ago. They maintain custom wooden shoe molds for specific custom-ers, and then a single shoemaker cuts the leather and hand builds shoes on a bench, one pair at a time. They charge as much as $5,000 a pair for shoes, a high price by any standard—in an industry that is predominated by much cheaper offerings from highly automated manufacturers around the world.

Rolls Royce, founded in 1906, is another example. Other than using automation in their paint processes, they still build cars one at a time with a few craftsmen. It can take as long as six months to build a single car. Yet, some of their vehicles sell for more than $600,000 without any options.

And where I now live (Fayetteville, Arkansas), Herman's Rib House has changed owners a few times, but strategically it operates much the same as when it was founded in 1964. Same crackers and salsa, same potatoes and steak offerings with their uniquely named "gear" salad. Same high prices at lunch and dinner. They aren't catering to calorie counters or those who want low-cholesterol or gluten-free offerings. And yet, the place is always packed every day at lunch and dinner.

Our building and development company, by the way, initially followed a strategy similar to the British shoemakers, Rolls Royce, and Herman's. Whether it was a new home or a rebuild, we used time-tested materials and methods. The same carpenters did the framing and the finishings. We used wood windows and doors, wood siding instead of Hardie Plank or vinyl, real rock instead of factory-made rock veneer, metal bathtubs instead of plastic, and copper plumbing instead of PEX.

Our houses sold before they were finished nearly every time at the high-est prices per square foot ever achieved in the area. It was only when we started to stray from this strategy and ramp up production that our profit-ability declined.

28

The Fundamentals for Selling Anything

T here's evidence to suggest that sales came naturally to me, but I also can assure you that there are skills anyone can learn to improve in this vital aspect of an organization's success.

While my experience in sales dates back to my days hawking bicycles on the street corner by my childhood home and grew as I expanded to motorcycles and cars, my greatest lessons about selling came when I landed my first job after grad school.

I was twenty-two and one of the youngest employees in a small executive search and management consulting firm in St. Louis. Mike Latas, my boss and the firm's founder and owner, had helped Xerox create and implement its national sales training program, and my three years of learning from him about business-to-business sales was a formative time in my career.

Over the next forty years, I continued to learn more and more about sales, and much of what I've learned applies regardless of what you are selling.

For instance, if you want to sell anything, you first need to decide who you are trying to sell to. You need a list. As obvious as this may seem, many so-called professional salespeople do not start with a good list of potential clients or customers. What organizations could be buyers for what you are selling, and who in those organizations could make or influence the decision to buy? This has to be your starting place.

Next, remember that selling is a numbers game. It takes a certain number of calls to get through to the person you are calling. It takes a certain number of conversations to get a meeting, a certain number of meetings to make a proposal, and a certain number of proposals to make a sale. Given enough activity, the probabilities will bear out certain results, so you know that the more calls you make, the more of your product you will sell.

Not everyone is a natural seller. Many people are afraid of it, feel that it has to be a win-lose process, or that it requires dishonesty. They are naturally reluctant to fully engage in selling. But if you embrace the idea that selling is all about helping, you will find that you become much more effective at it. If you, as the salesperson, help your clients or customers get what they want or need, you are helping them, not harming them. Knowing that selling is helping is critical to your ability to do it.

It's also critical to build strong relationships built on trust because clients and customers have to trust you before they will buy something from you. They won't trust you if they don't know you and like you, which is why effective salespeople ask lots of questions to get their buyers talking about themselves. Effective sales professionals also share information about themselves—sparingly and appropriately—with their clients or customers.

These relationships aren't always sales-driven. You have to check in with clients and customers every so often just to talk. Having no agenda whatsoever beyond seeing how they are and what's happening in their lives is an incredibly effective way to cement relationships with them, helping them to better know, like, and trust you. And, of course, more often than not, new opportunities to sell will become apparent.

At some point, of course, you have to ask for what you want. No client or customer will buy anything from you if you don't ask for the sale. I learned this lesson when Mike called us together one morning in the conference room and said we needed cash. He told us to ask for a retainer or advance payment from every potential new client we spoke with, but if we couldn't get one, the fallback position would be to work for them anyway.

A few days after, I was talking to a potential new client in New Jersey who had a need for our services. I quoted him a fee for the job and then did what the boss told us to do and asked for an initial payment before we could start. I was fully prepared to quickly cave in on my request and tell them we would go to work anyway when the client surprised me and asked where to send the check. Years later, when I started my own business, I got advance payments from every client, which proved crucial to our ability to bootstrap our growth.

Weak salespeople, meanwhile, give everything away. One of my mentors in the architecture and engineering business taught me that it's easy to sell a dollar for 85 cents. At that time, we had a partner who bragged about selling $3 million in services, but we lost money on every project he sold. If you over-rely on discounts and price reductions, you may sell a lot, but you may be harming your business over time. Not only will your firm not make what it should, but you will also jeopardize future profitable sales due setting a pricing precedent.

Selling is a skill that can be learned. The problem that many people have is that they never get the training they need to master the basics and overcome their misconceptions. That's a shame because learning how to sell can help in every aspect of your business and personal life.

Overcoming the Myths of Marketing

By now, you might have picked up that I'm a big fan of marketing as a tool for building a business. While sales are vital to the success of any organization, they must be complemented by effective marketing if a business is to grow.

So you won't be surprised to know that I've always been baffled by how many entrepreneurs and small business owners won't or don't use marketing. I've even seen companies that provide marketing services that won't employ the same tactics they espouse for their clients.

When I hear owners proclaim that "word of mouth is the best marketing," my first thought is, "Oh—so you don't do any marketing?" They typically are clinging to a fantasy that some miracle will happen, and their businesses will take off. Meanwhile, they struggle. And the longer they wait to start marketing, the worse their situation gets and the less they can afford to spend money on marketing.

Business-to-business enterprises that do little to no marketing end up with only one tool to get more business—personal selling. There's nothing wrong with personal selling except that the business becomes entirely dependent on a few people who can do it.

This creates three problems: First, it slows growth because there are only so many hours in the day to sell. Second, it increases the risks for the business because the best sellers could leave for another job, get sick, or become demotivated due to personal or family problems. Third, a dependence on personal selling—particularly if the owner or owners are the primary salespeople—devalues the business.

Still, many owners invest way too little in marketing. Why? In my experience, it's because they buy in to five common myths about marketing.

They don't believe marketing works. It's common for me to hear owners say things like, "We tried it once and it didn't do a thing for us." When you ask what they did, it usually involves some kind of a lame print advertising campaign, a sponsorship of a Little League team, or some kind of weak social media marketing effort that involved posting either blatant advertising or too many pictures of employee birthday parties. None of these things was likely to produce results—and certainly not as one-shot efforts—but that was their experience.

Unless you've invested in a legitimate marketing campaign and given it time to produce results, you will never know how effective it might be. On the other hand, if you talk to other owners who have invested in marketing efforts (like me), you will hear their stories as proof that it works.

One of the reasons my consulting, publishing, and media company, Mark Zweig & Associates and then later Zweig White, was so successful and grew by 30 percent annually for thirteen years in a row is because we heavily invested in direct mail. We spent an average of 13–14 percent of our total revenue on direct mail. Every year, we increased our spending on direct mail, and every year we had a commensurate growth increase in our volume. Our firm was profitable every year of operation and became a real brand in the business because we consistently spent on marketing and promotion.

They say they can't afford it. Every dollar spent on marketing increases expenses and reduces their profits, these owners will tell you. They don't understand that it is irrational and unrealistic to expect to grow faster than their industry's norm without spending more on marketing than their competitors. Marketing is what I like to call an "off balance sheet" investment.

They don't know how to do it. Not everyone who owns a business has a business degree, and many have had no business education whatsoever. These owners may buy into the idea, but they don't know where to start. That makes them vulnerable to unscrupulous or incompetent marketing firms or consultants, which leads to poor results and a bitter taste that lingers in their mouths for years to come.

Look for firms or people who have a real track record of success. Talk to their previous clients or employers, and ask about specific tactics they used and the results they achieved. Marketing people can be good at selling themselves, so practice due diligence because you don't want to hire someone who is learning at your expense.

They are too modest and feel self-conscious about marketing. I have seen many cases like this, particularly with people in the professional services industries that fifty years ago had credos that prohibited marketing and advertising. Those habits are ingrained.

Ziplining to Higher Furniture Sales

Barry and Eliot Tatelman took over Jordan's Furniture in 1973 when it had only five employees, and they immediately implemented a growth strategy for the company that their grandfather had founded way back in 1918.

Not only did the brothers open new stores in the Boston area, but they also aggressively promoted their business in traditional and non-traditional ways. They starred in their radio and television ads, becoming cultural icons in the area by spoofing popular movies. And in the 1990s, they began to expand with what's become known as shoppertainment experiences like a Mardi Gras–themed showroom and a $2.5 million Motion Odyssey movie ride.

They sold so much furniture along the way that they attracted the attention of Warren Buffett. In 1999, they sold the company to Berkshire Hathaway, fueling even more promotions and growth. Now their stores feature attractions like an enchanted village, an indoor ropes course, ziplines, and an IMAX theater.

The company is also known for promotions connected to the Boston Red Sox and Boston Bruins. They have often offered rebates or even full refunds on purchases if a team or player achieved significant feats, like pitching a perfect game or winning the World Series or the Stanley Cup. In 2007, for instance, they wrote rebate checks to around twenty-four thousand customers because the Red Sox won the World Series.

Both brothers remained with the business until Barry Tatelman left in 2006 to pursue interests on Broadway and in Hollywood. Eliot Tatelman, in his seventies as of this writing, remains as president and CEO, although there was one report that he had lost his strength after inadvertently cutting off his famed ponytail in a misguided attempt to give himself a quarantine haircut during the pandemic.

I don't pretend to know how much Jordan's Furniture had spent on promotions through the years, but this much I do know: It was worth it.

There are many things, however, that one can do marketing- and promotion-wise that are not braggartly! The current trend toward content marketing is all about providing useful information to your clients or customers and not trying to sell them anything. This can be in the form of original research, whitepapers, videos on how to use a piece of software or equipment, and anything else that is helpful and valuable. Your options are unlimited, and pretty much any business can use this tactic.

They think they are marketing with sporadic social media posts. Many small business owners and entrepreneurs put very little strategic effort into their social media marketing efforts. They mix their political messages in with cat videos and company employee birthday parties and then tell you they are using social media. Using it poorly, I'd say! In fact, sometimes it is so bad it hurts the business more than helps it.

The bottom line is this: Marketing is essential.

Getting Stuff Done

When you examine the careers of people who have accomplished a great deal over their lifetimes, one thing is apparent: They got things done—lots of things—even when they didn't have to. High achievers aren't waiting for someone to tell them what to do. They are self-motivated toward productivity.

Many self-motivated, elite performers have egos that demand they keep up and keep achieving. They also have a fear of letting anyone down. This personality trait, this drive to achieve more, more, more, is probably either born into us or inculcated by our parents. But I've also found that highly productive people typically practice certain strategies that turn self-motivation into productivity.

For instance, they overcommit. I realize that might sound like bad advice, and I'm not saying that overcommitment is the key to happiness or self-fulfillment. But it is one way to get a lot done.

I speak from experience. Just a few years ago, I was running two high-growth companies, teaching two classes at the Walton College, and serving on several boards of directors. I also had multiple development and construction projects underway and was writing more than fifty articles a year. On top of that, I have four daughters, the youngest of which was in kindergarten, two ex-wives to support, and a collection of more than twenty vintage cars and motorcycles, most of which needed work.

I didn't need to motivate myself. There were fires to put out every day (which is reinforcing when you succeed in doing so) because I was so prone to overcommitment. Overcommitment is one way (and I'm not saying it's the best way) to accomplish a lot. In fact, as I note in chapter 31, one of my regrets is the negative impact overcommitment had on my leadership.

Another way to consistently get things done is by continuously reevaluating your priorities. This has been particularly important since the pandemic because more people are working from home, and they are more personally responsible for managing their time. In many cases, they have more time for work because they've cut out the daily commute and gotten rid of a bunch of extraneous meetings. With that comes the need to use the time well. I always know the three to five most important things I have to get done each week, and I will make sure I accomplish those.

For me, accomplishing those things includes working off a good old-fashioned to-do list, which I find is unfortunately necessary but always useful. Many high-achievers I know still make these lists and check them off. My wife—an avid iPhone, iPad, and MacBook user—still likes to keep her to-do list on paper. She keeps that list taped to her vanity mirror and checks off what she gets done with a pen.

The form it takes doesn't matter. The point is you are working down the list of tasks that are related to your most important goals.

A to-do list is part of a structure that keeps high achievers focused and accountable. As someone who was a manager of his own businesses and pretty much the captain of my days, I have found that self-accountability comes from sharing my goals with everyone in the organization. I want to set a good example and can't expect others to be super-productive if I am not myself. I also share my to-do list and priorities with my spouse so she knows what I have to get done. She can and does help hold my feet to the fire. This is important.

In addition to systems like a to-do list, I also believe a structure to our daily routines is essential to our productivity. I like to get up early, and I find that the time between 6 and 9 a.m. is most useful for writing or grading. I take a quick lunch and try to get in a one-and-half to two-mile walk during the best weather time of the day. And I like to wrap things up by 5:30 or 6 p.m. if I can, so I have time to spend with my family.

Everyone is different. My old business partner, Fred White, who is an amazing accomplisher of complex long-range projects (he writes software today), used to work from about 10 a.m. to 10 p.m., six days a week, and then he played basketball on Sunday. Know yourself and when you are most productive, and then set a schedule accordingly.

When you take care of everything you can take care of to make yourself highly productive, there's still at least one other strategy you can use—getting help from others.

This is easy if you are a manager and have direct reports. You aren't asking them to do your work for you but to do their part in achieving your shared goals.

Even if you don't have people who are paid to support your work, you can solicit help from other people if you can get them enthusiastic about your project. I learned this at a very young age when I would enlist my friends to help with prepping a car for paint or doing an engine swap. Those who get a lot done have a way of bringing others in to support their cause, whatever that might be. Of course, if you expect to do this, you, too, need to help them with their efforts when you're needed. That's just the way it is!

The Life and Lessons of Leadership

T he success or failure of a new business often comes down to the founder's ability to lead others where they all want to go. If you get everything else right and lead poorly, chances are your business won't thrive because you won't have many employees or customers who are following you.

There are hundreds of books on leadership, many of them with wonderful frameworks, principles, laws, and models. What do I have to offer that they don't? Maybe nothing, but I can speak from forty-plus years as a student of business, management consultant, business owner, and college instructor.

What I know comes from experience, but much of it aligns with the best of those books you can read, and I think you can apply most of the lessons I've learned to just about any business situation.

Sharing My Regrets

Let's start with a few of my regrets as a leader. While I don't let my mistakes take up too much of my mental real estate, I do believe it's important to acknowledge them so that I can learn and not repeat them in the future—especially when it comes to leadership. And if you can learn from my regrets, then perhaps you won't have to make them yourself.

I wasn't open enough to my team's new ideas. I was so certain of our mission and strategies that I was very intolerant of anything that ran counter to them in any way. I was also resistant to changing systems that I felt worked. Our prior consistent growth and profitability were always my justification for my resistance to change. I'm sure I turned off some good people and shut out some good ideas because of that.

I was too judgmental of certain employees. In some cases, a single infraction of the rules—written or unwritten—was all it took for me to decide someone was not good and shouldn't be on our team. That was too harsh. I should have been more tolerant and less quick to pronounce a sentence. I also tended to micromanage people who had done something that made me lose confidence in them. That not only took up too much of my time and mental energy, but I also ended up demotivating the person.

I was so overcommitted that I failed to do parts of my jobs properly. This was undoubtedly one of my greatest sins. My philosophy, as I mentioned in a previous chapter, was that I would never have to motivate myself as long as I overcommitted and was a responsible person. I figured I would always rise to the occasion. But I wasn't always able to devote adequate time and attention to things that were the highest priorities for the business. I tried to do everything but ended up doing nothing very well.

I did not give anyone my full attention—ever! I was one of those people who would often sit in meetings and constantly look up things on my phone or respond to emails or texts. If someone was in my office, I might talk and listen while simultaneously doing stuff on my computer.

It's so rude. It's embarrassing that I was so disrespectful. I rationalized that I had to multitask because I was so busy. But the fact is, you can't treat other people like that and expect them to think you really care about them. As a wise person once said to me, "Your actions are so loud I can't hear what you are saying." Apropos in my case, for sure!

I let some cancerous managers and high-performers stay too long. You might ask why I would do this. There are three reasons. One, the manager and their team could be top revenue producers. Two, I always felt that I had to let managers run things the way they wanted to, or they would no longer be accountable for the performance of their team. And three, I avoided confrontation with my managers.

It's tempting to keep high-performers even when they hog all the credit and damage morale with a negative attitude toward others. But I would rather have a good performing team of ten with generally happy and motivated people than a rockstar and nine discouraged and unhappy people. And there is no valid justification for letting managers mistreat someone or making people feel so bad that they were demotivated or would leave the company.

Author Eric Chester once pointed out that rock stars are great if you like "egotistical front men who dress outrageously, show up late, perform stoned, smash pricey equipment, and trash hotel rooms." Maybe what we really need, he said, "are a few good roadies."[1]

I let some of my top leaders run off other good people because of favoritism. Promotion has to be based on merit, not how much your boss likes you—especially when there are other people in your unit who are outperforming you.

I will never forget losing one of our highest performers in a department because the manager simply liked someone else who worked for him. The other guy was more fun to hang out with whenever they were in the same city together, but he wasn't as productive, so the high-performer quit in a rage when he didn't get the promotion he deserved.

I was down on anyone who left the company. In some cases, I spoke disparagingly about people who left, especially if they wanted to start their own business or go to work for a competitor. In my mind (at that time), they were joining the enemy.

I never even went to the going away lunches because it made me mad that they had quit and upset that we were celebrating their departure. I thought we should be having "staying around" parties. But any of those people could have brought work back to us in the future or even come back to the company at some point. I doubt they ever considered it because I never acted like it was a possibility.

Advice for Leading Well

Good leaders realize that no one has to do what they are told. People have free will. It doesn't matter if they report to you or even if you own the business—if they don't like or respect you, they will not listen to you, and they won't always do what you want them to do.

When I think about my best advice for leading well, most of it centers on earning respect and trust, and much, if not all of it, would have helped me avoid most of those regrets if I had put it into practice sooner.

Lead by example. No one will respect you as a leader if you don't do everything you expect others to do. For example, in the architecture and engineering industry, partners often are frustrated when their people don't

1. Walt Rakowich, "Leading Rock Stars and Roadies as High Performers," August 12, 2019, https://waltrakowich.com/rock-stars-roadies-hire-high-performers/.

turn their timesheets in on time. Billing is based on these timesheets, and if they aren't completed, the firm cannot get paid. But do you know who I find are usually the worst offenders? The partners themselves! No wonder their people don't see the importance.

A do-as-I-do leadership culture also is reflected in a leader's work ethic. Leaders not only work hard and, when necessary, put in long hours, but they are also sensitive to others who are putting in extra effort and working hard. They acknowledge those workers with thanks. Again, they have no expectation that someone else will do something that they won't do.

Talk to people. Good leaders say "good morning" cheerfully to everyone. They ask the people they see in the hall or coffee room how their weekends were and how their family members are doing. They call and text their key people to check in when out of the office. They ask people out to lunch who are way below them in the pecking order. They walk around the office or store or shop floor. Talking to people is how you form relationships, and relationships are how you develop trust and commitment.

Listen to learn. Effective leaders focus on what someone is saying and devote their full attention while doing so. Try putting your phone down and actually listening to someone for fifteen minutes. Odds are—if you are a busy business owner or manager like me—that this will be difficult at first. But you have to do it if you want people to know you care about them.

Confront what needs confronting. This includes customers who are abusing employees, employees who aren't doing their jobs, and fellow partners or owners of the business who aren't carrying their weight.

Good leaders understand that other people need them to do this dirty work; if the leader doesn't do it, no one else probably will. If you are a leader, you may have to be the bad guy occasionally, and not everyone will always love you.

Be helpful. The best leaders pitch in and do what is necessary for the organization to fulfill its mission and meet its goals. They help other people do their jobs. They clear roadblocks for people. They get the resources and tools their people need to be more effective. They will do low-level tasks such as cleaning up the kitchen or a bathroom. There's nothing quite like showing everyone nothing is beneath you if you want to endear yourself to them.

Develop other leaders. It takes a lot of time and coaching and demonstration of how to do things to develop other leaders, and it doesn't always work out. When it doesn't work out, a smart leader will reallocate his or her time to help someone who may be able to learn from the lessons they have learned.

No one will be as good as you are at doing some of the things you have to do—at first. But given proper time, direction, and coaching, the person you are working with may actually become a better leader than you are.

Surviving a Crisis

The first order of any business is survival. If you don't do that—
survive—you can't fulfill your purpose-based mission, you can't
achieve your lofty vision, you can't solve all those problems for your
clients or customers, and you can't create all those great jobs in your community. Nor will you be able to enjoy success and satisfaction when things
turn around.

The best time to prepare for a crisis in your business is before it happens.

You might be living and working in a time and place where it feels like
the California gold rush of 1849, but we all know that the economy goes
through cycles. Those wispy white clouds that look so gentle on the hori-
zon can turn dark in a hurry thanks, or no thanks, to factors beyond our
control—political instability, rising interest rates, falling stock prices, wars,
natural disasters, global pandemics. None of us can predict the future with
precision, so it's best to be prepared—especially if you are a business owner
with employees and customers who count on your survival.

If times are good, here are six things to focus on at the first sign of storm
clouds:

Developing contingency plans. It might be smart to spend a little time
thinking about all the what-if scenarios that could develop. Deciding how
you might respond in advance of an actual problem can help you react fast
if it does occur.

Building your brand. The greater the familiarity of your brand with
your target customer group, the lower the risk is associated with their buying decision. That's what you want if the market suddenly declines.

Differentiating your business. When demand exceeds supply, it's easy
to forget how important this is. It's only when demand is *less* than supply
that differentiation becomes crucial. You want to have something no one
else sells.

Managing debt. When times are good, you might look to reduce debt and convert what debt you have to have into the longest-term, fixed-rate debt you can get. With rising inflation, you can expect higher interest rates. It's inevitable. So get yourself in a position where rising rates won't impact you significantly.

Securing additional credit. Get lines of credit based on your accounts receivable, inventory financing, or other lines of credit before you suddenly find yourself short of working capital.

Dumping nonessential assets. I define *nonessential* as anything that doesn't make you money but instead costs you money.

Of course, no matter how much you prepare, sometimes the storms hit you without warning. In 2020, when it became apparent that the COVID-19 virus was creating a global pandemic that would impact every sector of the economy, I had to admit that I was scared.

I was a business owner, creditor, and debtor. The business I owned had ground to a halt, and business for the firm that owed me money had slowed considerably. Everything was leveraged to the hilt and cross-collateralized.

Maybe I should have been a bike mechanic, I thought. *Maybe I should have been a postal worker. Maybe I should have just worked somewhere and kept my head down and lived in the $2,200 mobile home I bought when I was in college.*

The truth, however, was that I had no regrets. My businesses have given my family a pretty good life for the past forty years. But at age sixty-two and with two ex-wives and a family to support, I wasn't prepared for the pandemic. Usually, there are some warning signs when things are slowing down, and if you are astute, you can prepare. Not this time—and I wasn't alone. There were millions of other people—business owners large and small—who were in similar or worse situations.

What happens if we lose it all?

But I wasn't going to let that happen if I could help it. And I could. By taking action—and with sheer willpower—I knew I would fight (hopefully not to the death) to avoid going down.

Whether your business is threatened because of a pandemic, a recession, some other event that's beyond your control, or even mistakes you've made that have caused problems, there are always things you can do to right the ship and keep it afloat.

Some things will be specific to your business or industry, but here are some things in my crisis-management plan that apply to any business.

Operate in the moment. Successful entrepreneurs keep a long-range perspective. But when you shift to survival mode, you have to take things one day at a time. Each day you keep your doors open gives you a chance to turn things around.

This means paying super close attention to cash flow, deferring every cash outlay you can, and only spending money on things you absolutely need. No matter what business you are in, it's time to examine everything.

I like to look at the businesses I either own or am involved with from the standpoint of how many months we can go with a significantly reduced revenue stream. When it's only two or three months before we can't pay the bills, I'm worried. When it's five or six months, I'm less worried. If it's a year, I'm less worried still.

It's important to have realistic revenue expectations and to know exactly what your monthly costs are so you can make this quick but necessary calculation. Any additional costs you can cut or new revenue you can find extend the number of days you can survive.

It's also wise to make a list of all the assets you can dispose of and all the credit you have available. Sometimes things really aren't as bad as they seem if you inventory the resources that you could muster if needed.

Prepare for the unpleasantness. You have to make difficult decisions during difficult times. Who stays, and who gets laid off? Who gets paid, and who doesn't get paid? What will you be willing to do to bring cash in? How much new debt will you have to take on? And how much will you have to work—precisely when your family, who is probably scared and worried about their future, needs you the most?

Letting people go—especially good people—is one of the most depressing things I have ever had to do. I worked for a firm in Texas back in the 1980s and had to lay off more than thirty people in one day. It was awful. I went home feeling sick after delivering that news to people who had been there for twenty years and were making $50,000 a year when I knew they'd be lucky to get another job paying $5 an hour.

It is also not pleasant telling people you owe money to—trusted suppliers and service providers who either sold you something or did something for you—that you can't afford to pay them.

Make personal sacrifices. Now is not the time to live high on the hog. If you are serious about keeping your business alive and not going bust, you will have to do things you don't want to do.

Give up your daily Starbucks. Drive a cheaper and more economical vehicle. Sell your collection of whatever. Cancel the family vacation. Rent out your vacation house. Rent out your basement to another family. Cash in your profit-sharing fund. Sign up for more debt and guarantee it personally.

If you want to keep the machine that feeds you alive, you will need to feed it. That means taking out less, living on less, and putting in more money precisely when you will have less of it to put in.

Take care of your family. A major threat to your business, no matter what form it takes, is depressing and stressful, and that affects your family.

They will worry about their future, and they will worry about you, so you need to give them the time and attention they need, and you need them to do the same for you. Talk about it and give them a realistic view while at the same time not scaring them. Remind them that none of your stuff really means anything as long as you are all healthy and have each other. Stuff can be replaced (or maybe shouldn't be replaced even if you can one day do so).

Get sleep and exercise. You need your energy, and you need a clear head to deal with the tremendous stress of what you are going through. It's more likely that you will have these things if you eat and sleep. Otherwise, your judgment may be clouded, and your emotions run out of control—neither are good things when you are facing a financial crisis.

Keep out the garbage. All successful people have some friends who are only there because of your status. If that status declines or if you need help, that is when you will find out who your real friends are. Fake friends will abandon you. Real friends will be there to support you. The more quickly you identify your real friends, the sooner and better you can support one another.

It's particularly important to talk to friends who have been through difficult times themselves. No executive coach or therapist is going to suffice here. You need someone you can identify with as having been in your shoes. They will help calm you because they survived. They will also hopefully be able to give you specific advice on how to avoid disaster.

On the flip side, get off social media. All it will do is make you unhappy to see everyone else buying new stuff when you are worried about keeping what you have. Or seeing them going out to fun places or going on great vacations while you are either working or staying home, stressed beyond belief. Social media also exposes you to an incredible amount of negative information and bad news. Save your time and mental energy for what's important—real relationships with real people.

Let go of your ego. Owning a profitable and growing business—one that may even bear your name—is definitely an effective way to glorify your ego. But contracting, selling off stuff, telling people you can't pay them—those things will be a blow to your ego. You better learn to take those blows. You will have to endure many of them. Those who can't do what they must for their businesses to survive will be out of business—and maybe for good.

Look for opportunities. Tough times often bring opportunities for those who can see them and take advantage of them. A recession, for instance, is a good time to hire great people who have been laid off or are unhappy at struggling competitors.

It's also a good time to buy assets at low prices. The most profitable projects ever done by our firm, Mark Zweig, Inc., started with the acquisition of bank-owned properties during the last recession. Even if you don't want or need real estate, a recession can be a great time to buy tools and equipment for a manufacturing business, kitchen equipment for a restaurant, or anything you need that can help the performance or value of your business.

A recession also can be a great time to acquire a competitor's business. They could have good people, clients or customers, and valuable locations. And the owners might be so anxious to get out that they will finance the entire thing to a qualified buyer with a successful track record and proven knowledge of their industry (that's you).

If nothing else, tough times provide an opportunity to do some housekeeping. If business activity dies down and the pressure of daily performance declines, it could be a great time to replace the POS system, change processes that improve quality or customer service, or fix things in the business that need fixing. These opportunities may not be there when the system is stretched trying to meet demand during a boom time.

Pay attention to marketing. When times are tough, especially when they are tough for everyone, as was the case during the pandemic, you cannot keep doing the same things you always did and act as if nothing has changed. Everything has changed!

During the pandemic, I regularly saw television commercials that were clearly made before the crisis and social media posts that made no acknowledgment of the situation or that were more of what everyone else was posting (screenshots of Zoom meetings, pictures of pets, etc.) How about more original stuff on how people are using your products or services, specific actions you are taking to protect workers and customers, helpful information for other businesses, and promotion of new products or services that your client and customer base need?

If you don't want to see a decline in revenues, you may need to redouble your marketing and promotion. Spending more on marketing is the opposite of what most companies do when faced with a downturn. What better time to turn up the volume than when your competitors are doing just the opposite? That makes it easier for your message to be heard.

Listen to employees, clients, and customers. Probably the single most important thing you, as a small business owner, can do right during tough times is spend a lot of time talking with your stakeholders. If you are going to make it, you have to know the fears, frustrations, problems, and worries of your internal and external customers, and then act quickly to do anything you can that helps them.

Ownership and management must be on the front lines. It's not the time to be a general, working miles from the battlefront.

Reevaluate your life priorities. The decisions you made in the past—the good and the bad—are what got you where you are. Tough times are a good time to reevaluate those decisions.

Are you living a balanced life? Do you have good relationships with the people you care about? Do you control how you spend your time and who you spend it with? Do you have too much stress? Do you have too much stuff? Have you gambled too much in terms of the business risks you have taken on?

These and many more questions should be raised and answered, so if you need to make changes, you can start making them right now. And hopefully, you won't make the same mistakes or kinds of mistakes going forward because life (hopefully) isn't over. Today is always the first day of the rest of your life. Get that life going in the direction you really want it to.

Protect your reputation. Don't make excuses, especially if worse comes to worse and you have to close the business. Accept responsibility, and make a plan to pay your debtors.

Also, be very careful of appearances, such as driving a fancy car during or post-meltdown. I remember a developer who went out and leased a brand-new Porsche Turbo Cabriolet at the same time he defaulted on tens of millions in loans from area banks and didn't pay subcontractors. It upset a lot of people.

Your reputation is the most crucial asset you have. If you can maintain it, you will have another chance to come back. Many people have done so.

Remember: This, too, shall pass. Life has its ups and downs, and you might find yourself in a down period for you—a big one. But it won't last. Times will get better.

Sometimes, with human nature being what it is, we must experience the valleys to fully appreciate the glory of being on a mountain top. And, in fact, tough times often make us and others around us better.

Maybe your businesses will be less fat, more attuned to your clients' and customers' real needs, more efficient in your work methods, and better at using the technologies you should be using. Maybe you (and others who experience the tough times) will all be a little less materialistic, a little more prudent, and a little more willing to devote resources to helping others.

Making Management Transitions Real

One of the most overlooked aspects of creating a sustainable business is developing and executing on the management transition. Without that, the organization can't survive the inevitable departure of its founders or other key people. And those people eventually will depart. They will die, get sick, retire, leave for other jobs, or move up to other positions inside the organization. There has to be someone ready to go who can step into the specific roles being vacated when that happens.

While most business owners I know recognize this reality and the importance of developing leadership and managerial pipelines for the future, many organizations don't do a good job actually planning for such transitions. Just saying in a strategic plan that transitions are important doesn't make them happen. Making the transitions real—and making them effectively—takes specific actions.

For instance, I've found it essential for every manager or key employee to identify and name their successor. If they don't have someone in the organization, recruiting such a person has to be on their list of priorities. You have to insist this happens throughout the entire organization.

You also need to invest time in training your successor. And while the organization has a responsibility for providing some of this training, the bulk of the responsibility falls on the person who the successor will someday replace.

Identifying and training successors, of course, takes time. There may be other roles the successors need to fill in preparation. Some transitions can take three to five years, which is why you have to start the process right away.

I'm a planner. I hired my future successor in one of my businesses five years before he took the reins as CEO. It was part of the understanding when I hired him that he would succeed me. He worked in all of the different areas of the business and with many different clients. Over time, he assumed more and more responsibility. When he finally took over, it wasn't a surprise to anyone. While I won't say the transition was completely seamless—we had a few rough patches along the way—eventually, he found his footing, and the company is achieving new levels of growth and profitability as a result.

The work, by the way, doesn't end once the transition takes place. In fact, it's even more important to coach the successor once they've moved into the new role. Don't try to keep doing your old job if you have moved up or out of the organization, but give the new person the time, attention, and support they need to succeed. That includes public displays of support for the new person and the decisions they are making, even if you disagree and are privately telling that to your successor behind closed doors.

Even if you disagree with the person's decisions, accept the fact that no one will do the job exactly like you did. This is one of the most difficult truths in the succession processes. Your successor will do some things better than you and some things not as well. But they will undoubtedly do things differently from how you did. That's OK. Give them a chance.

If you made a mistake, however, own it and make a change. Despite everyone's best intentions, management transitions don't always work out. If this becomes apparent, you will need to act. Don't wait so long that the damage done from leaving the wrong person in the job exceeds the damage caused by reversing a decision.

How effectively your organization handles these critical transitions will greatly determine its long-term success. It won't happen automatically. You need to take the steps necessary to make an effective transition a reality versus just a fantasy.

Recognizing the Signs of Owner Burnout

Not long ago, I had a revealing conversation with a friend who is in his mid-fifties and has owned a business for almost thirty years. He was telling me about a meeting he had the previous day with a potential client. And not just any potential client but one of the biggest and best clients he might ever land for his business.

It was the type of meeting every entrepreneur covets. And, yet, here's what my friend told me: "Honestly, I struggled with my attitude under the surface."

The more we talked, the clearer it became that he was battling burnout.

There's no shortage of discussion in the business world about employee burnout, but you don't regularly hear much about burnout involving business owners. Yet, as my friend could attest and as I can confirm from personal experience, it's very real and far more common than many people might think.

I worked with the owners of thousands of privately held companies when I was a management consultant in the architecture and engineering industry. And each year, I assign my Walton College students a consulting project where they help small businesses find ways to increase revenues, increase profits, reduce risk, and increase the value of the business. So I regularly interact with business owners in my role as a faculty member, and I've come to see the signs of owner burnout.

The signs indicate that the owners have lost interest in their companies. They feel powerless. They are depressed. They may develop relationship problems with their spouses and business partners. They are demotivated. They disengage from the business and, in the most severe cases, from life. Sometimes, they shut the doors on their businesses and never come back.

I can relate. I still work every day in a number of businesses and jobs, but I'm probably not as driven to succeed as I once was.

How can successful people who own and run their own businesses—living the American Dream by almost any standard and who, theoretically, are in control of their destinies—experience such burnout?

There are many contributing reasons. Even if you are just starting out and full of passion and zeal for your career, it's worth looking at those factors now, so they don't catch you by surprise later.

You are addicted to your work. Workaholics can get a lot done—for a while. The problem is that their entire life revolves around their job. And when something bad happens at work, their whole world is shattered. Their history has been one of accomplishment after accomplishment and success after success, and any failure or setback can be devastating. That can lead to instant burnout.

Entrepreneurs often overcommit at the expense of their families. They work long hours at the office and are glued to a computer or phone when at home in the evenings or on weekends. It all leads to unhappiness, and that leads to burnout, not to mention pain in their personal relationships. I won't say that overcommitment to work alone was the cause of two failed marriages in my case, but it was certainly a contributor.

Your self-image is completely tied to the business. Many entrepreneurs include their name in the name of the business, so their ego is directly hitched to the success of the enterprise. Even if the owners' names aren't on the business, they often are well-known in their communities, and their identities are linked to their company. Any bad news, bad press, failure, or public setback has the potential to be tremendously demotivational.

Most of us have something bad happen to us or our businesses at some point along the way. Sometimes it is devastating. Even when we survive it, we get shaken and don't want to go through it again. We stop doing what we should be doing to keep our businesses growing and instead pull back.

I have seen a number of entrepreneurial privately held company owners make decisions to expand their businesses—opening a new office or new location for a retail business, for instance—and when it didn't work out (for any number of reasons), they concluded geographic expansion was no longer an option because of that one bad experience.

You are a control freak. Owners who struggle to delegate almost always experience burnout because everything goes through them. They can't get away from businesses because they don't trust anyone else to do anything properly. They usually end up with a crew of paralyzed "yes" people—or worse—no one working for them. They begin to feel trapped by their own business, and they feel powerless to do anything but react. This can lead to burnout.

You got into the wrong business in the first place. People end up owning and running a business for many different reasons, and not all of those reasons stand the test of time. Some inherit their business or get pushed into it reluctantly by a parent or spouse. Others get into it because they think it will be lucrative. Some simply misread the signs—they think they will enjoy the work but discover later that they don't.

The reasons are irrelevant. What is relevant, however, is that their lack of real passion and interest in the business leads to burnout when they are only doing it because they think they have to or just for the money—not because they enjoy it and are fulfilled by taking on the challenges.

I never experienced this situation, but I did grow tired of the development and construction business, in part due to the ethical climate of the industry. That's when we decided to exit.

Circumstances in your life change. Life-changing events can cause business owners to reevaluate all of their priorities. Oftentimes, business owners who suffer the death of a family member, get divorced, or go through a painful recession that requires a lot of tough calls decide they want to live the rest of their days differently. That may not include spending their time and attention on a business like the one they own.

I always caution my students when they tell me that they want to own a bar or restaurant that the work hours required to keep that business going may not be an issue when they are young and have no other commitments but could be a real problem for them later when they have a spouse and family.

And this doesn't just apply to bars and restaurants. When I was in a consulting business, I had to travel pretty much every week and missed a lot at home. Many people don't really think about what success in that business means when they start or buy a business. It can all lead to burnout.

As you get older, your risk tolerance also tends to decrease because you have more to lose and have limited time to make it up. When I started my primary business with $1,000 nearly thirty-two years ago, I had very little to lose. We had a $154,000 house we bought with only 5 percent down and no car payments or other debts of any kind. That changed over time.

If you are successful and fortunate, you may end up with a lot of investments and assets sufficient to retire on if you want. Let's face it, the closer you get to the clock running out, the more conscious you become that you don't have unlimited time. And there's nothing quite like a health scare to get one to reevaluate their priorities. Once again, the awareness of limited time makes you think hard about how you really want to spend it.

People problems wear you down. Dealing with employees, suppliers, and customers is enjoyable when things are going well, but it can wear you out when it's not. I was talking with a business owner friend of mine the other day—he's very successful and has been for a long, long time. Instead of worrying about how he could meet his seven-figure payroll, he was preoccupied with two good people in one of his ventures who didn't get along.

Your goals in life change. Entrepreneurs often start with goals that involve building value in their businesses and personal wealth for themselves and their families. At some point, however, they come to the realization that making more money and acquiring more stuff is no longer gratifying. We all only need houses that are so large, and none of us can drive more than one car at a time. We can only go out to eat seven nights a week and go on vacation so often.

Sometimes business owners can feel trapped by all their stuff because it costs so much and takes so much of their limited time to maintain. A few years ago, we owned nearly $20 million in real estate, around twenty cars, ten motorcycles, and a giant house with a pool and a 6,400-square-foot garage/car shop. It was ridiculous. Just getting more cars or a larger house or anything else material wasn't motivational at all.

While I eventually aspired to less when it came to material possessions, I aspired to more of other things. Like other business owners, after achieving a certain amount of material success (and that varies by person), self-actualization (remember Maslow's hierarchy of needs?) became more of a motivator.

I had an amazing career as a management consultant in the architecture and engineering industry, and I put on hundreds of seminars and gave hundreds of talks all over the country. Then in 2005, I started teaching at the University of Arkansas, both at the Sam M. Walton College of Business and, a year later, at the Fay Jones School of Architecture. While it was always a goal to do something like this, it became a bigger and bigger part of my life as I found teaching young people extremely rewarding in many new ways.

These things happen to many entrepreneurs. Just being known as someone who is successful in business is not enough. They want to do other good things. They want to go on a mission, start or lead a nonprofit, or teach, for instance. But these things take attention away from the business. If owners feel stuck with the business, they cannot pursue these other interests, and that leads to burnout.

I have always said that both the best thing and worst thing about owning your own business is that you have no boss. You should have a lot of freedom because of that. But it often doesn't work out that way. The business can become a trap.

The best time to start a business is when you are young because you will need every bit of energy, enthusiasm, and willingness to sacrifice to succeed. At the same time, nothing says you can't change direction or pick a different path in life. That is OK, too. If that desire strikes you, however, don't think your business won't suffer. And if you ignore your feelings and instincts and just keep doing the same things, burnout may very well be the consequence.

Cashing Out the Value

uilding value in your business—and cashing in when you exit—is
one of the primary distinctions between someone who is an entrepreneur and someone who is a small-business owner. All those years
of hard work and self-sacrifice are supposed to pay off in the end.

But do they? The answer is, "It depends." So much depends on you,
the owner, and whether you've prepared your business and yourself for
your departure. Many things can go wrong. Successfully selling a business
is rarely simple.

Here's my advice to owners considering an external sale as an option
for their exit:

Plan ahead. Don't wait until it's too late. "Too late" is when you are
sick or dead or have a need to leave the business driven by factors you
can't control. Once you decide to sell and start taking steps to make that
happen, you'll probably need a year or so to actually execute a transac-
tion. It may take much, much longer, however, to ready your business
for a sale.

Ready your business. I will never forget a Dallas-Fort Worth–area engineering firm whose owner wanted to sell and move to San Diego. Before we
could even try to sell that company, he needed a new business plan, a new
organization structure, five key roles filled, and a wide variety of financial,
HR, and marketing problems fixed. That took a year to accomplish. Then,
and only then, could we start marketing the firm to prospective buyers. We
did eventually sell it for a very good price.

Seek the advice of competent accountants and attorneys. I could say
this until I am blue in the face, but you need qualified accountants, attorneys, and other advisers to help sell a business. Not all CPAs have extensive
experience in minimizing the tax consequences of a business sale. Even
fewer attorneys have experience in the sale of businesses, and fewer still

have experience with businesses in your particular industry. Experts with the right experience will be worth whatever you pay them.

The worst people to help you through the sale are your regular accountants and attorneys. They probably aren't qualified, and some may even throw up barriers to the sale because they know they'll be losing a good client (you) after the sale.

Have a history of outside accountant-prepared financial statements. Audited statements are best, reviews second best, and compilations third best. Any of those are much better than internal statements. And buyers will want to see both income statements and balance sheets.

Have good info on all of your assets. If real estate is part of the deal, include an appraisal of it. Have a detailed inventory list. If you are a service business, be ready to share your client list and backlog of work. Buyers need to know what they are buying. When sellers don't have this information, it does nothing but slow down or sabotage the process.

Be realistic. You aren't going to get paid entirely in cash at closing. You aren't going to sell for twice what you are really worth. You are going to have to stick around for a year or two or even more after the sale. You won't make as much money post-sale as you made when you still owned the company.

On top of that, things will change, no matter what buyers might promise. And one thing you can count on is that you will likely no longer be the ultimate boss, which can be really hard for some people to accept.

These things may seem obvious, but a lack of experience with selling businesses results in some sellers having wholly unrealistic expectations and being naive about the process.

PART IV

Write This on Your Mortarboard

Graduation caps have become works of art at many university commencement ceremonies. Creative students use the square mortarboard top as a canvass for all types of clever designs and messages. Some paint colorful scenery or the school's mascot, while others hot-glue everything from flowers to cupcakes.

Then there are the messages, some inspirational and others more whimsical:

All it takes is faith, trust, and a little pixie dust.
To infinity and beyond.
Mischief managed.
Live long and prosper.
Oh, the places we'll go.

Perhaps my personal favorite was the student who wrote "Help! I'm in debt!" and included a QR code to her Venmo account.

As a teacher at the Sam M. Walton College of Business, nothing is more gratifying to me than to see students graduate and then go on to achieve their dreams in life—whatever those dreams might be. That's why this final section of the book offers some parting advice for students and recent graduates.

How to Find Success in Your First Job

T he focus of this book is on entrepreneurship, but I realize many students won't begin their careers by starting a new business. That step may come later, but the journey often begins by working for someone else.

So, what can you do in your first job to improve the odds that you'll create the best trajectory for your entire career? Perhaps these tips will help.

Learn about the company. It is shocking to me how many new employees don't know anything about the business they are working for. When was it founded and by whom? What are the major strategies? What is the firm's history, and what events inside and out shaped what the firm is today? Where is the firm going? Who are the people at the top, and what are their backgrounds? Knowing this type of information helps you engage with colleagues and with your work, which obviously is a good sign to an employer.

Learn first, suggest later. When you begin in a new role, you will inevitably notice things you would do differently. But don't push your fresh perspective too quickly. Learn how the company wants you to do things before making suggestions on how to change things. There may be good reasons why things should change, but there also may be good reasons for why they are done the way they are. When you are new, you lack the perspective that comes only from experience. New grads who are too quick to find fault with the ways they are being told to do things can look arrogant to supervisors, and you don't want to look arrogant (or be arrogant, for that matter).

Be responsive. Return all calls and emails promptly, including those that come in after hours. I have often found that the higher you go in the organizational hierarchy, the quicker people respond to their requests. But managers at all levels greatly appreciate someone who responds quickly because it shows they are conscientious and interested in their work.

Blooming Where You Are Planted

Kelsey Hensley, one of my former students, graduated from the Walton College in 2009 with a degree in economics and immediately stepped into a horrible job market. She explored several options and even went so far as to pay for her own airfare to go see a client in Florida, but she wasn't getting any job offers.

Eventually, she interviewed for a job selling freight services over the phone for J. B. Hunt Transport. The interviewer, however, thought she'd be better suited for an opening the company had in human resources, and Kelsey accepted that offer.

Even though that wasn't what she thought she really wanted to do, she threw herself into it and learned all she could about the logistics business. That led to her next job at Federal Express and then to a role as director of finance and accounting for a steel company. Finally, she bought BGS Fulfillment, a third-party logistics firm in Memphis. Later, she merged BGS with NovEx Supply Chain to become a bicoastal third-party logistics player.

All of her experience came together in transportation, logistics, and warehousing, and she owned her own business. She's also on the Marion, Arkansas, city council, and she and her husband will soon be opening a brick oven pizzeria there.

Like many college graduates, her journey took several turns she never expected. But at each twist, she worked hard and made the most of the opportunities, and that was a significant key to her success.

Put in your face time. Even though most of us can work from afar thanks to the electronic tethers of our phones and laptops, there's no substitute for being there. Being the first person in the office and one of the last to go shows that you are all-in and want to get ahead. While I am aware there is much more to life than work, working lots of hours early in your career can pay huge dividends later. It's typically at this point in life when you have fewer outside obligations. Take advantage of that time because there will come a day when you can't work so much. Work ethic—and perhaps even more importantly, the impression of it—are critical to your early recognition and success.

Watch what you put on social media. Your boss or bosses are probably on social media just like you. Sharing your political ideology—no matter how passionate you are about it—can easily backfire in our divided and polarized society. Gross or bad-taste humor can reflect poorly on you. Too many posts showing the parties you have been to or vacations you are going on can look bad to your superiors. And if you are having doubts about your career or problems at work, don't put that out there! Managers also are likely to notice when employees post on social media during work hours, so don't give them a reason to believe you aren't working while you are being paid to work.

Stay off your personal phone at work. There are times when you might need to make or take a personal call while at work, but don't allow non-emergency calls to take priority over work. For example, I have gone to the offices of newer graduates to speak about critical work matters only to spend several minutes waiting because they stayed on a personal phone call way too long. I have also walked clients through the office while an employee was on a personal call within earshot. The employee knew we were there and still didn't get off the phone. It was not a good impression!

Form relationships outside of your work unit. To advance in your career, you will need relationships with people outside of your work group, especially those at a higher level. You need to be known as someone who is friendly, smart, and willing to put yourself on the line, and having good relationships with people throughout your organization is crucial to that. Plus, you will have a more well-rounded view of the company you work for, which will help you do your job better and help you decide what new roles you might pursue.

Be a team player. Help others even when it's not required of you. Don't complain about your coworkers. Give them credit when you get recognized. When you take actions that indicate you realize the world doesn't revolve around you, you'll be seen as a team player because that's what you are. And management wants people who get along with and support the other people in the firm.

I realize some of these suggestions may seem old school to the new grads, but many of the owners and managers that you, as a new graduate, will work for are from the old school.

37

Working for an Entrepreneur

Many aspiring entrepreneurs find themselves working for an entrepreneur before they take the leap themselves and start or buy a business. That can be exciting and a good learning opportunity, but it also has its challenges. I know. I have been both the entrepreneur and employee working for one at various points in my life, and here's some of what I've gleaned from those experiences:

Entrepreneurs are terminally distracted. They are on their phones constantly and rarely pay full attention to what is going on around them because they are so focused on what they are doing. It may be hard to get their attention, and when you do get it, they might quickly forget about conversations or decisions they participated in making.

Some have attention deficit disorder (ADD). They bounce around like balls in a pinball machine from one thing to another. It may be hard for them to focus on anything for more than ten minutes. That can be frustrating if you need them to do something that is tedious or time-consuming yet necessary.

Entrepreneurs can be stubborn. They think they know better on some subjects than everyone else. It can be difficult to change their minds when you disagree with their position on something. They didn't get where they are by quickly embracing the reasons why something won't work. And they may interpret disagreement as disloyalty. That can be difficult to negotiate.

Entrepreneurs focus on entrepreneurial goals. They are working to build long-term value, for instance, versus maximizing profitability. Not understanding this very basic fact—that the entrepreneur has a different orientation from businesspeople who are seeking shorter-term results—can lead to frustration and dissent at the top. You might see an unwillingness to deal with a problem when, in reality, the entrepreneur is working on solving a completely different problem.

Entrepreneurs love people who show their commitment. They are fully engaged in their work and want to see what they perceive as that quality in others. That means showing up at the office on weekends, occasionally staying late, and quickly responding to phone calls, texts, and emails at all hours of the day and night. People who don't show a willingness to do these things may be quickly written off.

Entrepreneurs are unconventional people. They may dress differently. They may act weird. They may say things that others could find offensive or don't understand. They may not always appreciate individualism in others, but they want to project it themselves. Being recognized, being able to grab attention, and having a unique identity may all be part of their identity.

These realities about entrepreneurs mean it won't always be easy or fun to work for them. But while you may not want to spend your entire career working for an entrepreneur, you can learn a great deal from the experience.

38

Parting Words

The parting advice I typically share with graduates isn't just relevant to graduates. It's not only good for them as they begin their careers, but it's also good for the rest of us—including me.

One thing I value about my work as a teacher is that it gives me an opportunity to remind myself of all the things I've learned in my journey so that I'm less likely to repeat my mistakes. Whether you are just starting or, like me, you are in the later stages of your journey, never forget these lessons as you wrestle with the daily challenges that are inevitable in life.

Joy from the Journey

The destination is frequently anticlimactic, so you had best learn how to get joy from the journey. I say that as someone who set a lot of goals for himself and achieved them—not as someone rationalizing why I didn't accomplish what I set out to do.

While it is good to keep looking to the future, don't forget to take stock of the good in your present situation. I'd guess there is plenty of it. I missed out on too much along the way, and it took me a long time to figure that out.

Nobody Knows the Future, So . . .

Some industries will do well, and some clearly won't, but no one knows what the future will be. So pay attention to what people want and what their problems are, and use some common sense in evaluating where you will invest your time and talents.

Society has big needs and big problems. Everyone has to eat. Everyone needs housing. Everyone needs power (electric, solar, fuel, etc.). Everyone needs health care. We are all spending more time in our homes.

Exercise is a big deal. Cooking is popular. Home entertainment is hotter than ever. Home offices are the norm.

The pandemic created many new opportunities, and business is all about creatively finding solutions and filling the needs people have—be they real or perceived.

In addition to looking at industries that are doing well, pick an industry you love. That may be the most important thing. I was fortunate to spend much of my career in an industry—architecture and engineering—that connected my passions. While I was the "business guy" or one of the business guys in the firms where I worked or became an owner, I always worked with creative, intelligent, and ethical people. There may be industries that are fundamentally more lucrative, but the A/E business never got boring, and I got to spend my time with such great people. How much was that worth? A lot.

Low Overhead, Less Stress

I know what it's like to be a poor college student. I also know what it's like to be an overly indebted married professional.

When I got out of grad school at twenty-two, I had nothing beyond a '72 Chevy van with a worn-out clutch, a 1976 Honda CB550 four, and a 1964 New Moon mobile home that my girlfriend and I bought for $2,270. I was dirt poor, but my college and grad school were paid for, and I only owed my mom $100.

Two years later, I was making more money than ever, but I was house-poor—living in a new home we built with a payment that was nearly all my wife and I made each month in our jobs. We couldn't even afford to furnish it! I hated it and never made that mistake again.

The more you can delay gratification early, the more dividends you will gain later. You will have options that other people—the ones who loaded up with car payments, credit card debt, and expensive living quarters—won't have.

Choose Your Partners Carefully

Be careful who you team up with, in business but especially when it comes to marriage.

There are no guarantees in life, of course, but that doesn't mean we should be smart about our relationships in life. In business, we call it due diligence. In our personal relationships, especially when we're young, our emotions can blind us to even asking the right questions, much less paying attention to the answers when they aren't the answers we want to hear.

I can't tell you who to date or who to marry, but I can tell you that your personal relationships will have an impact, for better or worse, on every aspect of your life, including your business.

I got together with my first wife when we were eighteen. We got married at twenty-four. I loved her dearly, was married to her for nearly twenty years, and had two amazing daughters with her. But she had a lot of problems stemming back to a really tough childhood that she could not shake. They proved to be her undoing, and eventually, she had a complete breakdown with significant addiction problems.

It was very hard on my oldest daughters and me to go through this, and it set us all back greatly. I had to turn over my business to my business partners because I had to focus on taking care of my family. Thankfully, I now have a wife I can count on and who loves me and is my real partner in all things. Pick your mate carefully.

Bad Habits Are . . . Bad

There's a reason bad habits are described as bad—because they aren't good for you. Drinking too much, smoking, using drugs, compulsive spending, gambling, eating too much, and all the other things your mother warned you not to do will, if you do them, drag you down. Some of them will even kill you.

If you have any of these tendencies, fight them. You aren't a helpless victim. You can beat it. You must control your urges if you want the quality of life you should have. Seek help when you need it—not only from friends but also from professionals. But while professional resources may be helpful, don't ignore the importance of who you hang out with. Your friend group can have a huge influence on you. Try to spend time with people who boost you up versus drag you down.

Maintain Your Relationships

Friends and family become more important the older you get. Don't forget your parents, many of who helped their offspring get through college by making significant personal sacrifices. And remember your friends, too. I am lucky that I still have a few good friends from my childhood. My wife has many. It makes life a lot richer.

To have and maintain decent relationships, there are times when you have to take the initiative. You must be the one who calls to check on the other person instead of waiting for them to call you. You must ask them over for dinner or out to lunch. You must jump in and volunteer to help out if they have a problem with a child or are struggling with a move.

Don't Spend All Your Time on Work

Hobbies provide an outlet for the stresses and pressures of work. For me, having worked in white-collar jobs since I was twenty-two, restoring motorcycles, cars, and houses provided something where I could see tangible results. That is very gratifying.

Hobbies can be a source for great friendships while providing satisfaction you just can't get from your job (which will undoubtedly provide you with other satisfactions).

Tune In, Give Back

A well-lived life is an ongoing process of learning and giving.

So keep learning. Stay tuned in to current events because they clearly impact you and your business. Watch the national news. Read the paper. Read books. Listen to podcasts. Go to talks. Take a class. Keep learning inside your discipline and outside of it.

You can be a lifelong learner, or you grow stale while the world changes around you. In my experience, the former yields a better, more fulfilling life and career.

And last but not least, take everything you learn and all the success you earn and give it back to others. Help someone who needs it. Give your time and money. Be a big brother or sister. Call on the elderly neighbor next door before you go to the store to see if they need anything. Teach a class.

Donate to your favorite charity. Go on a mission trip. Give back to your alma mater. Look around at the needs you see and do something to meet them—just like you do in your business.

When you get older and you think about the most rewarding experiences in your life, my guess is they won't be the luxury vacation you took or the car you bought that you always wanted. They will be the times you helped someone and knew you were doing good.

Here's a list of organizations that support entrepreneurship. While most of these are specific to the region where I live, some are national or even international.

- Small Business Development Centers—The US Small Business Administration provides a wealth of online resources for entrepreneurs who want to start or grow a business, and it also operates centers all across the country. These centers are frequently tied to state universities but not always. They provide free or low-cost counseling and training to business owners (https://www.sba.gov).
- Arkansas Small Business and Technology Development Center— This Arkansas-based center is funded in part by the US Small Business Administration (SBA) and in partnership with the University of Arkansas at Little Rock and the University of Arkansas at Fayetteville (https://sbtdc.uark.edu/).
- Startup Junkie—This nonprofit provides entrepreneurs with no-cost, one-on-one consulting; hosts events, workshops, and programs; and provides access to capital and talent (https://www.startupjunkie.org/).
- The Brewer Family Entrepreneurship Hub—This interdisciplinary collaboration venue offers coworking space and a training center for University of Arkansas students, faculty, alumni, and new and early stage entrepreneurs in Northwest Arkansas (https://entrepreneurship.uark.edu/places/the-hub.php).
- The Social Innovation Initiative—The University of Arkansas offers programs that give students opportunities to explore how entrepreneurship and innovation can address social and environmental problems (https://entrepreneurship.uark.edu/programs/social-innovation.php).
- The McMillon Innovation Studio—This is an interdisciplinary program for students at the University of Arkansas, but area business leaders can get involved as mentors for the design teams (https://mcmillonstudio.uark.edu/).

- The Startup Village—Selected companies received office space that includes shared services such as a conference room, kitchen, printer, Wi-Fi, phones, and mailboxes (https://entrepreneurship.uark.edu /places/startup-village.php).
- Plug and Play Tech Center—This venture capital firm and business accelerator based in Sunnyvale, Calif., has corporate partnerships around the world in a variety of industry verticals. While it has offices in Germany, Singapore, and Shanghai, the home for its supply chain and logistics vertical is in Northwest Arkansas. This program helps connect startups with established companies (https://www.plugandplaytechcenter.com/arkansas/).
- Vistage International—Peer groups make for wonderful counselors and advisors. Vistage matches leaders with seasoned CEOs in their industry who can provide insights and advice based on similar experiences. You can go to https://www.vistage.com to find groups in your area. I am a coach with Vistage Northwest Arkansas, and you can connect with us at https://www.vnwa.net.
- Chamber of Commerce—Chambers of commerce provide help for the businesses in the communities they serve, and in most cases it is worth joining and playing an active role in your local organization.
- Universities and colleges—The Sam M. Walton College of Business at the University of Arkansas is a great example of a school that works closely with industry to create mutually beneficial relationships. If the universities in your region aren't actively doing this, encourage them to do so. It will benefit their students and their communities.

Mark C. Zweig has been an entrepreneur since his youth in Kirkwood, Missouri, and maintains a passion for building companies and helping other leaders succeed in their businesses and in life.

He started his career selling bicycles on the street corner of his childhood home and by mowing lawns around his neighborhood. By the age of twelve, he got his first "real" job working at Kirkwood Cycle Shop. From there, he worked for three other bike shop owners in about ten different stores. He also bought and sold cars and motorcycles.

As a child, Mark thought he wanted to be an architect, but he soon was seduced by the world of business. He went to Southern Illinois University at Carbondale, where he earned a business degree and an MBA, and then worked for consulting firms in St. Louis, Memphis, and Fort Worth.

Much of Mark's professional career has been spent architecture, engineering, and construction industries. He has been a partner, investor, and board member for several firms and was the founder and chairman of Mark Zweig & Associates, a management consulting, publishing, media, and training firm that is now known as Zweig Group.

When Zweig Group was sold in 2004 to a private equity firm, Cardinal Growth, Mark relocated to Fayetteville, Arkansas, where he had started teaching entrepreneurship at the Sam M. Walton College of Business. He also founded Mark Zweig, Inc., a Fayetteville-based design, development, and construction firm. He remains an entrepreneur-in-residence at the Walton College and also is chairman of Vistage Northwest Arkansas.

Mark has written several thousand articles over the years and authored a number of books. He still writes a weekly editorial for *The Zweig Letter*, read by owners and managers of AEC firms worldwide, and has done so for more than thirty years. He also regularly contributes to the "Walton Insights" blog on the Walton College website and to the *Northwest Arkansas Business Journal*. He has given hundreds of talks at a wide variety of national, state, and local events.

Additionally, Mark has been a founder or cofounder of several private companies, including a reading clinic, a baby products company, and a bike shop. He has served as an outside director or advisor on the board of directors of more than a dozen private companies, served on three university boards for two different universities, the Fayetteville Chamber of Commerce board, and he is currently on the board of directors of Miyamoto Relief, a nonprofit that provides a wide range of projects in third-world countries struck by natural disasters.

Mark's interests—besides his businesses and family that includes five daughters—are in art, architecture, antique and special-interest cars, motorcycles, and bicycles. He has modified and restored a wide variety of cars, hot rods, and motorcycles, and he has owned more than four hundred cars and three hundred motorcycles, including a number of prize-winning restorations. His houses have appeared in *Better Homes and Gardens, At Home in Arkansas, Renovation Style Magazine, Citiscapes Magazine,* and many others. He has received many awards for his buildings, including Developer of the Year, Best Historic Restoration, and Best Adaptive Reuse.

Mark is married, has four daughters and one stepdaughter, and lives in an old Victorian house on the edge of downtown Fayetteville, Arkansas. When he isn't teaching classes or working with students or Vistage members, he can be found on his front porch.